THROUGH THE TEARS

KAREN CECILIA JOHNSON

THROUGH THE TEARS

CARING FOR THE SEXUALLY ABUSED CHILD

BROADMAN PRESS
NASHVILLE, TENNESSEE

4260-62
ISBN: 0-8054-6062-4

Dewey Decimal Classification: 362.7
Subject Heading: CHILD MOLESTING
Library of Congress Card Catalog Number: 92-18651
Printed in the United States of America

Scripture quotations marked NASB are from the *New American Standard Bible.*
© The Lockman Foundation, 1960, 1962, 1963, 1968, 1971, 1972, 1973,
1975, 1977. Used by permission.

Scripture quotations marked KJV are from the *King James Version* of the Bible.

Scripture quotations marked NIV are from the Holy Bible, *New International
Version,* copyright © 1973, 1978, 1984 by International Bible Society.

Library of Congress Cataloging-in-Publication Data

Johnson, Karen Cecilia. 1957-
    Through the tears : caring for the sexually abused child / Karen
Cecilia Johnson.
        p.   cm.
    Includes bibliographical references (p. 177).
    ISBN 0-8054-6062-4
    1. Parents of sexually abused children—United States.
2. Parenting—Religious aspects—Christianity.   I. Title.
HQ759.914.J64   1993
362.7'6—dc20   92-18651
                                                                 CIP

CONTENTS

Dedication

"For this child I prayed"
1 Samuel 1:27

I lovingly dedicate this book to my oldest daughter.
I pray that through your tears, God will heal your hurt.
My prayer for you has always been that you will become a
beautiful woman of God who loves and serves Him.

Acknowledgments

I am grateful for my husband's loving encouragement to attend Mount Hermon's Christian Writers Conference and begin to pursue my dream of writing a book. He also taught me how to use a computer and that is an accomplishment in itself! This book is the result of that dream.

I am thankful for the two beautiful daughters the Lord has blessed me with. I appreciate the extra help and hugs they would give me so I could write. Sometimes they would make dinner or play for awhile so I could write just a little longer.

Bonnie Wilkinson, MA, M.F.C.C., has been a mainstay of support and ideas. As she reviewed each chapter, she would send me helpful ideas along with a note of encouragement. I treasure those notes.

I want to thank Linda Johnson-Wood, Licensed Clinical Social Worker and Mr. Roger Cross, C.E.O. of Youth for Christ, for reading my manuscript. I appreciate the ideas and input I received from Jan Frank, author, speaker, and M.F.C.C.

I especially want to thank the parents who shared with me the hurts in their families from sexual abuse. I pray that together, our stories will help heal the hurts in others' families. A special thank you to the anonymous parent who helped me extensively with the legal chapter and reviewed and edited my entire manuscript.

As I reflect on this project, I don't want to forget to thank the countless family and friends who would inquire about my progress in writing. Without their support and encouragement, I'd probably still be wanting to write a book.

Introduction

No tears in the writer, no tears in the reader.
—(*The Figure a Poem Makes. Preface to Collected Poems*
[1939] Bartlett's, 750:3)

"It can't be true. It's not true. Even if it's true, I don't want to know about it." I listened as the conference speaker, Jan Frank, listed symptoms of someone who had been sexually abused. Red lights began to flash in my mind. My six-year-old daughter had many symptoms of a child who had been sexually abused. I couldn't believe what I'd heard. Heartbroken, I returned to my hotel room. Alone at last, I cried out to God. I sorted through the hundreds of thoughts racing through my mind.

My daughter had been in counseling for four months. Why hadn't anything been said about symptoms of sexual abuse? I couldn't believe something so horrible had happened to *my* daughter. Her innocence and carefree childhood had silently been robbed like a thief in the night, and I knew nothing about it. Terrified, I had to know the truth.

Secretly hoping my suspicions were wrong, I met with Jan Frank and told her about the symptoms I saw in my daughter. She said sexual abuse sounded like a possibility. Her answer wasn't what I wanted to hear. Crushed by her response, I buried my head in my arms and cried. Through the tears, I asked, "What do I do? How do I know who's abused her? How do I tell my husband? What if he's abused her?"

She replied calmly and lovingly. "Right now, you don't know. Pray that God will reveal the truth." She shared with me a verse in the Bible, Daniel 2:22, which says, "It is He who reveals the profound and hidden things; He knows what is in the darkness, And the light dwells with Him" (NASB). It is only through this exposure that a person can truly begin to face what has happened and begin the healing process.

She shared with me how to explain to my husband what I'd learned and the symptoms I saw in our daughter. She suggested I explain to him what I'd discovered and listen for his response. If he was willing to inquire further into this possibility without resistance, it would be unlikely he was molesting her.

That evening, with tremendous fear and trepidation, I reluctantly called my husband at home. I don't remember exactly what I said, but when I finished, there was silence on the other end of the phone. I waited, my heart beating faster, my palms sweaty.

Finally he spoke. "I guess we better find out about this."

Relief flooded my mind. I desperately wanted to hear those words. From that point on, my husband and I were a team in getting help for our daughter. I don't know what I would have done if he had not wanted to pursue information regarding sexual abuse. My book would certainly contain a different story.

When a person learns about a tragedy of any kind, being with someone who can love and support you through the immediate crisis is a tremendous help. I met a young lady earlier that day, and I talked and cried with her until late into the night. I never saw her again. When I called my husband, a very good friend was with him and available for him to talk to as well.

My husband and I immediately called our daughter's counselor. She said that her symptoms were the same as an abused child, but she felt they were simply developmental issues. She didn't think we needed to explore the possibility of sexual

Introduction

abuse since our daughter was making progress. We were angry! As parents, we had a right to this information.

Suddenly, our family life as we knew it was changed, shattered and broken with the devastation of possible sexual abuse. Fearfully and cautiously, I prayed for God to reveal the truth. I frantically ran to the library to devour every piece of information on sexual abuse I could get my hands on.

Unfortunately, most of the information was written for professional counselors or adult victims dealing with childhood sexual abuse. I only found one book about parenting a child who had been sexually abused. Ultimately, that became the reason for writing this book.

My husband and I felt alone and confused, struggling daily to find answers and information about parenting our sexually abused daughter. We had so much to learn by trial and error, endless hours of reading, and many more hours of tears and frustration. I had no idea of the rough road to recovery that lay ahead for each member of our family.

There were days I begged for a break. I just couldn't take any more truth, and the Lord would graciously give me a week or two to process the truth He had already revealed. The process of uncovering the truth, layer by layer, was excruciatingly painful. I didn't want to know any more, yet I felt I had to know more. Our lives became consumed with finding out information.

If you are reading this book, you may suspect or have discovered that a child you love with all your heart has been sexually abused. This child may be your own child, a relative's child, a friend's child, a neighbor's child, a child in your church, or perhaps your grandchild. I wish I could be with you in your home to give you a hug, cry with you, and tell you how sorry I am that you and the child you love are hurting. My heart goes out to you and the child. I pray this book will be an encouragement to you as I share my daughter's story, others' stories, the effects on the entire family, and the healing process—through the tears.

Two months into my research, I realized I also had many symptoms of sexual abuse. As I entered two years of counseling, I began to vividly recall being sexually molested from ages four to fourteen by a family member. I had repressed the memories because they were too horrible to recall. Now I had a dual role as a detective; I had to peel away layers of truth for both of us.

Perhaps you, too, have been the victim of sexual abuse and are now reliving your nightmare through your child's experiences. In that case, you have double work ahead of you. It may not feel like it now, but let me assure you that recovery for you and your child is possible. One in four girls and one in seven boys are sexually abused by age eighteen. That means that 25 percent of parents of daughters and 14 percent of parents of sons are devastated just like you and are looking for hope amid hurt—through their tears.

Most sexual abuse is passed on from generation to generation. You are choosing to help your child, and perhaps get help for yourself if you've been abused. I trust this book will help families break the generational sin of sexual abuse. You can know that the chain of sexual abuse in your family can be broken so that future generations will not have to suffer needlessly. As I told my mother, because my daughter and I were getting help, this will be the last generation in our family to be abused.

Although many books are available to help adult victims of childhood sexual abuse, this book is written especially for the caring adults and parents of sexually abused children. I trust this book will be a helpful guide for you in discovering how to best parent or help a child as he or she recovers from the trauma of sexual abuse.

You will find practical information on day-to-day management of the molested child. How do you handle running away, poor self-esteem, suicidal tendencies, and other problems your child has? Together, we'll look at parents in pain, the effects on marriage, siblings, and extended family. The suggestions on

Introduction

how I dealt with guilt may help release you from any false guilt. We'll cover every aspect of childhood sexual abuse, from symptoms, denial, anger at God, choosing a counselor, and discipline, to building trust, self-esteem, and legal concerns.

You will identify with the stories and situations gathered from hurting parents just like yourself. You may find it helpful to keep a journal of your thoughts and feelings throughout the recovery process. Sometimes when you are discouraged, reading through your journal and seeing progress will be encouraging. So grab a box of tissues, find a comfortable chair, and let's begin the road to recovery *Through the Tears*.

1

It Can't Be True: Symptoms of Sexual Abuse in Children

They brought me bitter news to hear and bitter tears to shed.
—William Johnson Cory, *Heraclitus. Translated from Callimachus*

> As I stood in the hallway, I looked longingly at my daughter's precious face in the row of pictures. I could barely think straight. I could hardly imagine what someone did to her to cause her so much pain at such a young age. I'm so scared. I don't want to know what happened, and yet, deep down inside of myself, I keep searching for the truth. (*Journal entry*)

I felt confused about what had happened to my daughter. Would I ever know? I felt like my family's lives were a five thousand-piece puzzle, and we only had three puzzle pieces, and God had all the rest. The counselor told me that healing would come as each piece of the puzzle fell into place. Sometimes when God revealed a piece, I would get a sick feeling in my stomach, then I would write the information and my feelings in my journal.

You may feel like your life is a jigsaw puzzle. You may have witnessed the act yourself by walking in on your child and the perpetrator during the molestation. A teacher may have suspected symptoms of abuse from your child's pictures or stories. Maybe you were told by someone else, like a social service worker. Perhaps the child told you himself.

Regardless of how you suspected or discovered a child was molested, you probably feel a wide range of emotions. You may feel overwhelmed, enraged, doubtful that it really happened, guilty for not stopping it, and very isolated. Your emotions are a natural reaction to trauma. After you first become aware of a child's sexual abuse, much of your life will seem to center around that concern. Please be assured that it won't be that way forever, even though you may feel that way now.

The Secret Is Revealed

It took great courage for a child to tell you what happened. Most children don't tell anyone, often because they think no one will believe them. One child said, "I told my mom and she said she never wanted to hear talk like that again." Children may not have the vocabulary to express what happened. They may speak in vague terms: "I don't like Mr. Smith anymore." If they get an equally vague response, they may not say anything more. Sometimes children may think they have told, but they aren't understood. For example, a child might say, "Mr. Smith wears funny underwear."

If children have been taught to always obey their elders because grown-ups know what's best, they may take to heart the abuser's assurances that "it's OK" or they may give promises not to tell, which they are afraid to break. "He told me it was our special secret."[1]

Many adults have a difficult time accepting disclosure of a sexual assault that happened a long time ago. Coping with the thought of a child carrying a burden alone for such a long time is hard. Parents can be tempted to believe it couldn't have happened or the child made it up; after all, the child didn't try to get help.

Many times, however, past problems begin to make sense. In our case, my husband and I had discussed our daughter's behavior over the years, but never knew she was showing us symptoms of sexual abuse. She was even in counseling, and we knew nothing about the abuse.

Do not blame the child as hard as this might be. His story may sound absurd, but try to believe him. In time, you will learn more details regarding the abuse. A child desperately needs to know that someone he loves believes him and loves him regardless of what happened.

Research indicates many children who report being sexually abused actually minimize the amount and type of abuse. Exaggeration is rare. Only two or three children per thousand make up the event of sexual molestation or exaggerate what happened to them.[2]

Telling about the abuse is often a very frightening experience for a child. The child doesn't know what to expect, may feel out of control, or may fear blame or disbelief. Many children feel consumed with guilt. A sexually abused child feels alone, not only within his family but within himself. He may be unable to create a place in his soul to cry his heart out.

You may want to hug the child and tell him you're sorry about what happened and assure him you still love him. Maybe you feel angry with the child or feel that he caused the abuse to happen. We live in an offender-protector society. Society wants to say that the victim is responsible. A child is *never* responsible for being molested. He is an innocent victim; the adult who made wrong choices is totally responsible. The current predominant attitude among clinicians and researchers is the total legal and moral responsibility for any sexual behavior between an adult and a child is the adult's.[3]

Right now, the child needs five assurances:

1. You still love him, no matter what happened.
2. You are sorry about what happened.
3. It's not his fault.

4. You will try to protect him from further abuse.
5. You will get help for him.

This chapter will help you define sexual abuse, types of sexual abuse, and molesters. An extensive list of physical and behavioral symptoms is included for you to evaluate the child. First, let's look at the term "child sexual abuse."

What Is Sexual Abuse?

The term "child sexual abuse" has been defined by the National Center on Child Abuse and Neglect as "contact or interaction between a child and an adult when the child is being used for the sexual stimulation of the perpetrator or another person. Sexual abuse may also be committed by a person under the age of 18 when that person is either significantly older than the victim or when the perpetrator is in the position of control over another child."[4]

Warning signs of sexual abuse may include both physical and behavioral signs. Often the child will not tell you about the molestation with words, but with a change in behavior. Since children are not usually able to tell directly, it helps to be sensitive to their signals.

After our research my husband and I identified more than twenty warning signs in our daughter. Our daughter cannot yet recount specific incidents of abuse. Her counselor said that our daughter had an incredible amount of rage. She feels whatever happened was preverbal. With the vast number of symptoms, and knowing she had been left many times with my perpetrator before I remembered my own abuse, we have no doubts that she's been sexually abused. When I see the devastation of her life, I know that her life has been scarred by trauma. Sometimes I believe God is protecting her from remembering events too horrible to recall. I do believe that some day she will become strong enough emotionally to be able to remember the events of her past.

One day, when I shared with her my own symptoms, she asked me, "Mom, do you think someone did something to me?" Even at seven years of age, she was already able to recognize many of the symptoms in herself. I answered that we didn't know for sure, but that we had reason to suspect something had happened.

Her tremendous fear of the water parallels the fact that my perpetrator began molesting me in the bathtub as a child. Looking back, we can see a progression of symptoms which occurred over the years she was left with the perpetrator. I would like to share with you some of the warning signs we saw in our daughter to help you realize the vastness of symptoms and potential ways that a child can react to abuse.

As a one-year-old, she would force herself to gag and throw up by forcing her hand down her throat. Masturbation began at two years of age, which is common in many children. However, in her case, the masturbation has continued for years. She would masturbate lying down on the floor, on the corner of her desk at school, and on our pets.

She began asking questions related to sex at a very young age. At the age when most children are just figuring out there are differences between boys and girls, she knew about sexual intercourse from all the questions she'd asked us. She uses seductive behavior with men. We have seen her act so seductively that men have had to move away from her because she made them feel so uncomfortable.

She began running away at age three and a half when she packed her suitcase and took off on her tricycle down the street. Our daughter has a tremendous need to control her environment. Just driving a different way home from church or school would upset her entire day. She would become frantic and ask, "Why are you going this way? We never went this way before."

Our daughter was fearful, especially of people dressed in costumes, like Mickey Mouse, Chuck E Cheese, and clowns. She was terrified of Santa Claus. Frequent nightmares kept our family up at all hours. At four and a half, she began wetting the bed almost every night, after being dry at night for more than two years. Six years later, this continues to be a problem. (See ch. 8: "Managing the Molested Child," part 2.) She complained about pain while urinating. We later discovered she had frequent yeast infections.

During kindergarten, we noticed an obvious personality change. In fact, we began to wonder if she was schizophrenic. In seconds, her behavior could change dramatically. For instance, we would be having a fun conversation and suddenly she'd start screaming and acting in bizarre ways. She would regress to the behavior of a two- or three-year-old when she was schoolaged. Sometimes she would sob and cry for no apparent reason. At this point we sought professional counseling for our daughter. We didn't know what was wrong, but we knew her behavior wasn't normal.

She has incredibly low self-esteem. She thinks she's fat and ugly when actually she's thin. Frequently she becomes obsessed with exercise and puts herself on a rigid diet. Childhood depression was difficult for us to identify, even though physicians told us she was depressed. Suicidal thoughts were expressed at times. She'd say, "I wish I was dead. I'm going to kill myself."

Difficulties with impulse control have caused many behavior problems at school and at home. Excitability, restlessness, making inappropriate noises, a short attention span, and inappropriate behavior are just a few annoyances we deal with regularly. At age seven, she was finally diagnosed with Attention Deficit Disorder (ADD), commonly known as hyperactivity. Somatic complaints like headaches and stomachaches were frequent.

Although our daughter was very outgoing, we found she had poor peer relationships and an inability to maintain friends.

She was picked on by kids in her class with regularity. Children can exhibit symptoms of sexual abuse in many different ways. These symptoms are cries for help.

Although some of the symptoms of sexual abuse are different in children than in adults, many of the symptoms are the same. Following is a list of warning signs found in children. Many children will exhibit one or two of these symptoms. Some of these symptoms may be a part of a child's normal development process, but a combination of several (four or more) might indicate a need for adult or parental concern. Key considerations are whether these behaviors are a dramatic change from a child's normal behavior and how obsessive the new behaviors become to the child.[5]

Warning Signs in Children

1. Fear of specific persons or situations/strangers
2. Nightmares, waking up during the night sweating, screaming, or shaking
3. Withdrawal (social or emotional)
4. Begin wetting the bed/change in sleep patterns
5. Personality change
6. Loss of appetite or other eating problems without a logical explanation
7. Eating Disorders
8. Unprovoked crying spells
9. Clinging to significant adult
10. Excessive washing/baths
11. Poor self-image/low self-esteem
12. Changes in type of fantasy play
13. Fear of being alone
14. Refusing to go to school
15. Running away
16. Attempting to control environment/fear of unknown
17. Early sexual precociousness: initiates sophisticated sexual behavior, promiscuity

18. Difficulties with impulse control
19. Complaining of pain while urinating or having bowel movement, indicating infection
20. Symptoms indicating evidence of physical trauma (abrasions or lesions) to the genital area
21. Somatic complaints: Develop frequent unexplained health problems, for example: recurring stomachaches, headaches, and pains in muscles and bones that have no logical cause or possible indicators
22. Depression
23. Expressing thoughts about death or suicide, or displaying suicidal actions
24. Self-destructive behaviors, for example: drug/alcohol abuse, suicidal gestures
25. One child being treated by a parent in a significantly different way from other children in the family
26. Arriving early at school and leaving late
27. Poor peer relationships
28. Bouts of asthma, choking, and gagging, possibly recreating the sensation of oral rape
29. Gynecological disturbances such as dysmenorrhea (painful menstrual periods) and amenorrhea (absence of periods) in adolescent girls
30. Abnormally early physical development
31. Masturbating excessively
32. Extreme fear of undressing
33. Symptoms indicating pregnancy
34. Regression to behavior the child has already outgrown
35. Suddenly not performing as well in school

When the University of Chicago's Jon Conte compared 369 sexual abuse victims with children who had not been abused, he found that the victims had more nightmares, were more depressed, had more problems in school, daydreamed more, and had more trouble remembering things. They were more "aggressive and fearful," less "rational and confident," and more likely to withdraw from the normal activities of life. Their self-images were poorer, and they were more anxious to please adults.[6]

You may realize a child you love exhibits many of the warning symptoms, but you know nothing about possible sexual abuse. You immediately question the child, but he says that no one has ever done anything inappropriate to him. Does this mean the child was not sexually abused? Not necessarily.

Children who were molested under the age of three will probably not have a conscious memory of the abuse. A child's ability to remember does not begin to develop until about the age of three. The symptoms will still be evident in the child, but he won't be able to give an account of what happened. Another possibility is that the child remembers, but has repressed the memory due to the trauma of the event(s). There's also a slight possibility the symptoms are a sign of developmental problems and not due to abuse. At any rate, a child with a number of symptoms will need help whether or not the symptoms stem from child sexual abuse.

Types of Sexual Abuse

Now that we've looked at many of the warning signs of sexual abuse in children, you will be saddened to know there are many different types of childhood sexual abuse.

Nontouching offenses may include verbal sexual stimulation, such as frank discussions about sexual acts intended to arouse the child's interest or shock the child, obscene telephone calls, exhibitionism, voyeurism, and letting down the bars of privacy so that the child watches or hears an act of sexual intercourse. Touching offenses may include fondling, vaginal, oral, or anal intercourse or attempted intercourse, touching of the genitals, incest, prostitution, and rape.[7]

"Incest is defined as any physical sexual activity between family members. A blood relationship is not required. The term 'family' is used in its broad social connotation as well as to describe the actual living arrangement of the involved persons."[8] Stepparents and unrelated siblings living together, often as a result of their parents' previous marriages, are included in the definition of incest. So are other relatives who do not permanently live with the child—uncles, aunts, and grandparents, for example. Abuse at home means there's nowhere to run for protection.

Pedophilia (literally, "love of child") denotes the preference of an adult for prepubertal children as a means of achieving sexual excitement. They seek sexual gratification from a child. Either girls or boys may be the sexual object. The range of actual activity may include any of the forms of sexual abuse, since the term "pedophilia" really indicates not a kind of activity but the fact that a child must be the participant-object in the activity. Most pedophiles rationalize that they truly love children. That's one reason they're so dangerous. In their public relationship with children, for the most part, they appear to be harmless, friendly, and caring.[9]

Exhibitionism (indecent exposure) involves the exposure of the genitals by an adult male to boys, girls, and women. The purpose of the exhibitionist is to experience sexual excitement and to shock or surprise the onlooker. Even though he may talk or call attention to himself, he does not usually make any other approach.

Molestation is a vague term which usually includes other vague terms such as "indecent liberties." Molestation includes such behaviors as fondling, touching, or kissing the child, especially in the breast or genital areas. It may also include engaging in masturbation of the child, or urging the child to fondle or masturbate the adult.[10]

"Sexual intercourse (statutory rape) with a child of either sex, including fellatio (oral-genital contact), sodomy (anal-genital contact) or penile-vaginal intercourse may occur without physical violence, through seduction, persuasion, bribes, use of authority, or other threats. The lowest limit at which a child is presumed to be able to give legal consent to intercourse varies from state to state from ages twelve to eighteen. Except for legal consequences, age of consent is of much less significance than the meaning of the individual experience for the child or adolescent involved."[11] In California, any sexual activity with a boy or girl between the ages of fourteen to seventeen is statutory rape. If the child is under fourteen, the offense is child molestation. For molesting children under ten, the penalities are even more severe.[12]

Rape is defined as sexual intercourse or attempted intercourse without consent of the victim. Unfortunately, even extremely young children, (under six months of age,) have been objects of rape; however, the majority of child rape victims are over five years of age.

Sexual sadism is the causing of bodily injury to another as a means of obtaining sexual excitement. Portrayal of sexual sadism is sometimes a part of child pornography. These scenes are not always "faked."

Child pornography is the photographic production of any material involving minors in sexual acts, which can include other children, adults, or animals. The distribution and/or exhibition of such material in any form, with or without profit, is considered child pornography, regardless of consent given by the child's legal guardian.[13]

One organization promotes sex with children. The Rene Guyon Society believes that child sex and pornography are natural. "Sex by year 8 or else it's too late" is its slogan. It claims to have 5,000 members in 50 states, including psychiatrists and legislators, all of whom are supposedly working toward changing the existing laws.

Child prostitution involves children in sex acts for profit. Generally, child prostitution uses frequently changing partners. This rampant practice involves boys as well as girls.[14]

Who Molests Children?

Contrary to popular belief, most sexual offenses against children are not committed by strangers. Eighty-five percent of the sexual assaults on children are by people known to them— often a relative, neighbor, or friend of the family who takes advantage of a position of trust over a period of time. Child abusers look and act like everybody else. Many of them are men and women with jobs and families, liked by their co-workers and neighbors. They are respected in their communities— the sort of people whose friends will say, "It can't be true. I know that guy. He's a nice guy." Many people still think of the sex offender as a stranger who lures children from school yards, playgrounds, and parks. However, most abuse appears to take place in the home of the offender or the victim, and in many cases this is the same place.[15]

What factors contribute to sexually abusive behavior? There are two general characteristics common to those who sexually abuse children. One characteristic is a lack of impulse control. The other is a confusion of roles, where the child becomes an object for the needs of the adult without the adult's recognizing either the inappropriateness or the inability of the child to meet these needs. Additionally, the practice of incest is frequently passed on from one generation to the next.

Other Factors to Consider

1. Prolonged or habitual absence of either the mother or the father from home
2. Assignment of a "mother" role to a daughter; for example, caring for other children, cooking, or looking after father

3. Stepparent or live-in boyfriend/girlfriend
4. Loss of the spouse by divorce, separation, or death
5. History of child abuse in the background of one or both parents
6. Conditions of overcrowding, alcoholism, drug addiction, or intellectual limitation of parents or child
7. Inability to establish normal social and emotional contacts outside the family because of eccentric belief systems, extreme poverty, or remoteness of the area in which the family lives[16]

How Common Is Sexual Abuse?

Current statistics show that one in four girls and one in seven boys are sexually abused by age eighteen. That means that 25 percent of parents of daughters and 14 percent of parents of sons are devastated, just like you, and are looking for hope amid hurt in parenting their sexually abused child. Female children are more often subject to sexual assault than young boys.[17] "Two million children run away from home each year, and up to half of them do so because they have been abused, primarily sexually. The average age of a runaway child is now 12 years, whereas ten years ago it was 15."[18]

I realize all this information is heavy and painful for a caring adult or hurting parent. Try to remember that you are beginning on a road to recovery. On a journey, you can only take one step at a time. Give yourself a pat on the back for taking those hardest first steps. In the next chapter, we'll discover the next steps in coping with the devastating news of a child's sexual abuse. Go ahead and keep that box of tissues near you. If you're like me, you'll shed many tears throughout the child's recovery.

2

Yes, It's True: Now What?

Thou art a soul in bliss; but I am bound
Upon a wheel of fire, that mine own tears
Do scald like molten lead.
—William Shakespeare, *King Lear IV, vii, 46*

As I held our beautiful daughter sleeping in my lap tonight, I wondered how she became so emotionally ill. She's so precious to us. I can't imagine how by seven years of age she has so many problems. (*Journal entry*)

Here I am again, brokenhearted. I just looked at my daughter's seven-year-old picture. Sometimes I can hardly think straight when I look at her precious face and begin to imagine what someone did to cause her so many problems. (*Journal entry*)

"It can't be true." But deep down inside, I knew it was. Perhaps you have also discovered or suspected a child you love has been sexually abused. Perhaps you're beginning to believe it is true. Emotionally, you may feel distraught, helpless, and confused. Thoughts are spinning through your mind, creating confusion, questions, and doubts. You may be physically exhausted from not sleeping and/or not eating. What should you do next? Take a deep breath, sit down, and try to relax. When I'm confused, I often pray to God and ask Him for guidance and wisdom.

Reporting the Abuse

You are in the beginning stages of dealing with the shocking and horrible knowledge of sexual abuse. Child sexual molestation and exploitation is the most unreported crime in the nation today. An estimated 90 percent of these crimes go *unreported.*[1] If you do not know whom to call, you may contact the national hotline at 1-800-4-A-CHILD.

My husband and I learned that just because we reported the abuse did not mean that we had to prosecute. That information helped in our decision-making process. Right now, you may not know what decisions you and your child will make in the future. However, not reporting a child molester only protects the abuser. It does not protect the child. Not reporting the abuse only perpetuates the sexual abuse and makes other children vulnerable. Check with your local child protective services regarding mandatory reporting laws in your state. You may be required to report your suspicion or knowledge of sexual abuse within a certain number of hours.

You may want to file a report. A social worker came to our home to ask questions and file a report. Please note that just because a report may be filed as "unsubstantiated" does not mean the child has not been abused. It simply means there is not enough evidence at that time for the police or social service departments to take any action.

Reporting child abuse can be separated into three components, each contingent upon the one preceding it: identification, investigation, and intervention.[2] Let's look at each of these components.

Identification

The basic vehicle for the identification of child abuse is the mandatory reporting statute. This statute includes the definition of child abuse, who must report, what agency is designated to investigate the report, and what immunities are offered, which will vary from state to state.[3] Information requested in the initial report usually includes:

1. The name and address of the child suspected of being abused
2. The name and address of the child's caretakers
3. The name and address of the child's parents (not necessarily the same as the child's caretakers)
4. The identified injury or reason you suspect abuse which led to the report
5. The name and address of the suspected perpetrator(s), if known
6. The names and ages of all other children within the same home (if possible)
7. Any other information which may be helpful[4]

The Investigation

If the investigation has been completed properly, the investigative data should allow the case worker to determine:

1. If the child is currently in danger in the home
2. If the child's injuries or the parents' behavior can be classified as child abuse under state law
3. What the success of therapeutic intervention might be (prognosis)
4. What treatment should be offered to the child, to the parents, and to the family unit[5]

Intervention

Intervention can be divided into two categories: voluntary intervention and involuntary intervention. The majority of treatment plans are implemented by a voluntary agreement between the child's parents and the department of social services. Voluntary intervention is used when the parents are willing to work through their problems; the reported injury to the child is not serious; there has not been a continual history of abuse; and the prognosis is favorable.

Involuntary intervention is used when the parents are uncooperative; the reported injuries are severe; there has been a history of past abuse; or the prognosis is poor and foster care or a termination of parental rights is indicated.[6]

Physical Examination

A physical examination can provide valuable information about the possibility of abuse in some cases. Physical trauma or injury has been found in 20 to 35 percent of suspected child sexual abuse cases. The percentage is low because the most prevalent form of child sexual abuse, fondling, often leaves no physical indications. Also, children experiencing more invasive forms of sexual activity often do not report the abuse until long after it has occurred. Conclusive physical indications are often no longer present.[7]

Even though physical indicators are present in only a minority of sexual abuse cases, most clinicians and physicians recommend a physical examination for each suspected victim. In some cases, a child may be willing to admit to less intense forms of sexual activity, but feels too embarrassed to say what other types of sexual activity, such as intercourse, occurred. For this reason, some physicians recommend all forms of sexual abuse be investigated during the physical exam, regardless of the initial complaint of the child.[8] The physical examination generally includes a thorough medical history taken from the parents and child. A detailed account of the sexual abuse and when it last occurred provides important information.

Medical procedures are frightening and upsetting experiences for children, particularly for a sexually assaulted child. In order to make this process as easy as possible, remember the child's perspective. Ask the doctor or nurse to explain to you and the child what is going to happen and why. Make sure the child understands at his own language level. Allow the child to ask questions.[9]

Another consideration would be the appropriateness of requiring or requesting that the siblings of a sexual abuse victim be examined. A number of fathers abuse more than one child. Some cases have been cited in which the father begins with the oldest child and abuses the other children as they reach a certain age. Although some incestuous fathers may sexually abuse only one child, they may physically abuse others. If other victims are discovered, they can receive needed attention.[10]

What do you do if a child is reluctant to be examined? Although it would be wrong to force a completely uncooperative child to have a physical exam, concerns about losing valuable evidence of the abuse must be weighed against allowing the child to return at a later time. Sufficient physical evidence may mean that the child will have to spend less time as a witness in a future court proceeding or may not have to appear at all.[11]

Does My Child Need Counseling?

When your child is physically ill, sometimes you take him to the doctor. Other times, like with a cold or brief flu bug, a trip to the doctor's office is not necessary. Sometimes your child is ill and you have no idea what is wrong, but you know he's sick enough to need a physician's diagnosis. The same is true regarding your child's emotional health. As a parent, you know your child better than anyone else. Does your child appear to have no ill affects from the abuse or is it obvious he's suffering emotionally? Do you realize something's wrong, but you're not sure exactly what the problem is?

You may want to consider seeking professional help if your child obviously needs help or if you're not sure. If you see signs of sexual abuse in your child, don't make the decision yourself. Get an evaluation. This way you can get feedback, and the burden is not all on you. Sometimes it's difficult to be objective regarding those we love.

Marriage, Family, and Child Counselor Jan Frank believes every sexually abused child needs counseling. Using evaluations, a professional will be able to give you guidance as to the possible benefits that your child would receive from counseling.

Perhaps you are a youth worker or friend who feels a child needs counseling. You may want to consider approaching the parent(s), sharing with them what you've observed and suggesting ways to help the child. Not all parents will appreciate your involvement, but many will respond positively. At least you can know you tried to provide help for the child and family. Please remember, you may be required by law to report your suspicions of abuse.

The psychological consequences of sexual abuse are too little understood. What is known is that, one way or another, most children do not emerge from such an experience unscarred. Victims of child sexual abuse often sustain damage that lasts many years.

The three most critical times in the life of a sexual abuse victim when counseling is most needed are: "1.) immediately after the abuse events; 2.) at the time of marriage; and 3.) when her own children near the age at which she experienced abuse."[12] There are several factors which seem most significant in judging the effects of any sexual abuse. Let's consider those factors in more detail.

1. There appears to be a significant correlation between intensity of trauma and a.) the age difference between the partners and b.) the amount of coercion involved.[13]

2. There is evidence that sexual involvement with a family member is more disturbing than sexual experiences with an unknown adult.[14]
3. There is some evidence that the younger the child is when the abuse occurs, the more severe the psychological disturbance the child is likely to manifest as an adult.[15]
4. The length of time over which abuse takes place, from a fleeting episode or multiple contacts over months or the degree of child participation.
5. The reaction of the adults to whom the child confides the story.
6. The consequences of treatment or legal intervention.[16]

Locating the right professional help for your child is a difficult and time-consuming process. Working with sexually abused children and their families is often a combined effort of individuals from legal, social service, and mental health agencies. Work with incestuous families may involve even more agencies. Finding the best counselor will save you time and money in the long run. After a negative experience with our daughter's first counselor, my husband and I learned some tips on interviewing and selecting a counselor.

To find a counselor, start looking in the yellow pages of your phone directory under Marriage, Family and Child Counselors, Children's Crisis Services, Psychologists, and/or Physicians—Psychiatry. If possible, talk with friends or acquaintances who have used counselors and get the names of professionals with whom they had positive experiences. Many times local churches have referral lists of counselors available.

Each time I needed to find a new counselor, I called at least ten to fifteen potential counselors. This takes a great deal of time but can be extremely helpful in choosing the best professional help for your child and family. There are many different types of professional help available, as well as the different fields of psychology. Let's look at the types of counseling professionals available.

Types of Counselors

Clinical Psychologists: Emphasize the understanding, diagnosis, and treatment of individuals in psychological distress. Clinical psychology is historically based on laboratory work that stressed experimental and statistical analysis. Most clinical psychologists develop competence in both diagnostics and intervention. The area of diagnostics includes individual interviews, psychological testing, and personality assessment. Intervention (the actual approach used to help a person) can include individual therapy, psychotherapy, group therapy, and/or marriage and family therapy.

Psychiatrists: Before they specialize in psychiatry, psychiatrists receive the training required of any medical doctor. After this, there is specialized course work followed by a period of psychiatric internship. The educational background of psychiatrists enables them sometimes to identify a physical basis for emotional difficulties. The psychoanalytical orientation still dominates much psychiatry. Psychiatrists are the only therapists who may prescribe medication.

Social Workers: Are trained to deal with developmental problems, life crises, and emotional problems in a variety of social situations. Almost all social workers are specially trained to conduct intake interviews in which they find out about the "presenting complaints" and about the person's general life circumstances.

Marriage and Family Therapists: Are relationship specialists who treat people involved in interpersonal relationships. They are trained to assess, diagnose, and treat individuals, couples, families, and groups to achieve more adequate, satisfying, and productive marriage, family, and social adjustments. The practice also includes child counseling. Marriage and family therapists are licensed psychotherapists.

School Counselors: If your child is schoolaged, you may consider contacting the counselor at your child's school. Many school counselors work with sexually abused children. Sometimes group counseling is offered for children with similar circumstances.

Religious Counselors: The world's first professional counselors were religious. Guidance from priests, rabbis, and pastors has a long tradition. The tradition is such an old one, in fact, that going to a religious counselor has a respectability the public has not yet extended to other forms of counseling. Many professional religious counselors receive training in contemporary therapies.

Once you have chosen the type of professional help you desire for your child, you also need to know some of the different fields of psychology available.

Fields of Psychology

Psychoanalysis: There are many theoretical assumptions underlying psychoanalysis, but the key ones include a belief that the nagging, neurotic problems we wrestle with as adults are the result of childhood experiences, usually unpleasant and usually beyond the reach of conscious remembering. These unresolved conflicts continue to provide the impetus for our failure as adults to learn, to love, and to work. Analysis involves getting at these unconscious dynamic forces, events, and conflicts so the person can understand them and begin to make informed choices about how he or she wants to live life.

Psychoanalysis tends to be more concerned than counseling with fundamental personality-structure changes. Frequently, psychotherapy is a longer-term process.

Behaviorist: The emphasis is on behavior change. Behavior therapy tends to address problems more specifically than psychotherapy and is less concerned with finding out the original cause of the problem.

Gestalt Therapy: Gestalt therapy focuses on the here and now, rather than dwelling on the past or the future. The key to gestalt therapy is the concept of "wholeness"—the development of an awareness of exactly where feelings are coming from, and through that awareness, developing conscious control over those feelings.

Types of Therapy Sessions

Play Therapy: This is a form of individual therapy usually recommended for young children. In play therapy, the guiding principle is that the child will express his feelings through play rather than through conversation. Some examples of play therapy are: Water play—time to experience "messiness" and opportunity to explore, to splash, to express oneself without the restraint generally necessary at home. Athletic play—a place where emotions, particularly anger, can be expressed safely. Doll house play—allows the most direct expression of the maltreated child's struggle at home. It is not uncommon to observe the child taking out frustrations and anger on the dolls. Dramatic play—helps children express and work through emotional struggles. Play therapy is the type of therapy our daughter began when she was six-and-a-half years old.

Art Therapy: Art therapy is one of the most effective ways of helping children who are suffering from sexual assault. A therapist may use an "artmobile" that contains paints, chalk, clay, and other materials. A child is invited to use whatever he wishes or is invited to work with a trained adult on a one-to-one basis. Many times a child's feelings can be recognized by what is drawn. This method is often a part of play therapy.

Individual Therapy: Individual therapy may be recommended for the child and/or for one or both parents. In individual therapy, the person meets regularly with the therapist.

Group Therapy: Group therapy consists of several people, usually four to eight, meeting with one or more therapists (usually one, sometimes two.) A typical goal in group therapy is to improve each person's skills in relating to others. In the treatment of childhood problems, a group may be recommended for the child (usually with peers) and/or for the parents.

Family Therapy: In family therapy, all family members meet with a mental health professional and discuss their relationships with one another. Procedures and duration of family therapy will depend on the family, its difficulties, and the therapist's theoretical orientation. Some sexually abused children come from environments that have contributed significantly to the distress they exhibit during or outside of therapy. In some cases, the sexual abuse provokes the preexisting distress of the child, and in others the sole source of the distress may be the child's environment rather than the sexual abuse. In other words, in the context of a myriad of other abuses, sexual abuse may have little additional impact on the child.

Child-Rearing Counseling: The parent(s) receive advice on how best to cope with their child. The goal of such counseling is improved parent-child relations and improved child behavior.

Inpatient Treatment: Treatment can be delivered in an "inpatient" setting, where the child lives most of the time at a hospital or school, although he may go home for visits. When a recommendation is made for the child to live away from home, parents must evaluate this recommendation very carefully. Parents need to be sure they understand the goals of the suggested treatment. We have discussed with our daughter the possibility of a thirty-day inpatient treatment program at some time during adolescence.

Twenty Questions to Ask a Potential Counselor

Now that you have chosen the type of counselor and field of psychology that you feel will best meet the needs of your child and family, here's a suggested list of questions I used to interview potential counselors by phone. You will want to have paper and pencil handy to jot down notes while speaking with each counselor.

1. Do you work with children who have been sexually abused? If not, ask for names of people who do and thank the counselor for his or her time.
2. How many sexually abused children have you counseled? How long have you been counseling sexually abused children? (Remember, you're looking for an expert, not someone to experiment with your child.)
3. Ask the counselor about credentials, membership in professional societies, and inclusion in any national listings.
4. What is the average length of time you spend counseling a sexually abused child? (This answer will be vague because so much depends on the extent of the child's warning signs and response to counseling.)
5. What is your professional training and degree?

6. What is your professional philosophy/field of psychology?

7. What are your personal religious beliefs? (This was particularly important to us.) Just because someone claims to be a "Christian" counselor does not mean he or she has the training and experience to help your child deal with sexual abuse. A person who means well can compound a problem by saying and doing the wrong things. At the same time, it is important to choose a person who respects and upholds Christian principles.

8. How do you communicate with the parents? How often?

9. How will I know my child's progress?

10. How do I handle questions I might have?

11. How do you feel about "patient confidentiality" in regard to the parents? (In California, parents have the right to all information regarding their children under eighteen years of age, except in areas dealing with sex. A parent signs a written consent for treatment, just like when your child visits a medical doctor. Check your state laws.)

12. In a crisis situation, are you available by phone to the parents? to the child?

13. What are your fees?

14. Do you offer a sliding scale for fees based on income?

15. Do you bill insurance?

16. Do you offer a discounted rate if I don't have insurance coverage?

17. What is the length of each counseling session?

18. Will we be allowed weeks off from counseling for vacations without having to pay for sessions?

19. What is your cancellation notice policy?

20. If the above nineteen questions are answered acceptably, ask to set up an appointment with the professional to discuss your child's specific situation. "When would be

a good time for an appointment?" Remember to ask what the fee for the first appointment will be. (Sometimes a counselor charges half the normal fee for a consultation.)

Believe me, I understand this procedure is very time consuming, but I found comfort in knowing I was at least beginning to *do* something to help my daughter. You, too, are trying to make the best decisions to help the child you love. I found counselors very willing to spend time on the phone answering my questions. It will take fifteen to twenty minutes to answer all twenty questions. If a counselor is unwilling to talk with you by phone, you probably will not have good communication with the counselor in the future.

After talking with our daughter, we decided to find a female therapist for her. You may want to consider how you and your child feel about a counselor of the opposite sex. We were more comfortable with a therapist who was the same sex as our child.

The Consultation Appointment

You may feel apprehensive and anxious about meeting a counselor for the first time. For a consultation appointment, my husband and I chose the counselor we felt best about after talking with that person on the phone. After the consultation, we chose that person for our child. However, if you have any doubts, take the time and money to pursue another consultation with a different counselor. *At the consultation:*

1. Explain briefly your child and family's circumstances. This can include your impression of how the child used to be and how he has changed. Try to recollect when the changes occurred and what else was happening in the child's life when the changes occurred.

2. Explain the process in which you decided to seek professional help. Explain what you have already done to help your child. You have probably already spent many hours trying to help your child.
3. Ask the professional how he can help your child and your family.
4. What process will he use to evaluate your child?
5. What types of programs will he be likely to recommend for your child and family? (i.e., play therapy, individual or group therapy, number of times per week, etc.)
6. What procedures will he use to evaluate the effects of treatment?
7. Be sure the professional explains and gives you a written copy of his policies.

Evaluating the Professional

1. Was he on time?
2. Were you greeted in a friendly manner? Were you treated with respect and courtesy?
3. Did you feel comfortable with the counselor?
4. Did he answer your questions in language that you could understand?
5. Did he communicate clearly?
6. Did you sense that your child would like this person?
7. Did you like the person? Was he transparent?
8. Did you feel like the professional could help you and your family?
9. If applicable, was the room conducive for play therapy? Were there toys and play items for the younger child?
10. Overall, did you feel like this person would provide the best therapy for your child and family?

If so, congratulations! Now you are ready to continue the process of seeking professional help. You may want the child to be a part of the choosing process. If there are two or three equally qualified professionals, let the child be the deciding factor. It is critical that the child has a counselor with whom he can establish rapport. If you find several counselors who would be qualified, you are truly blessed. Each time we searched for a counselor, we only found one we felt would be suitable.

Next, set up a time for your child to meet the potential counselors you've screened. We found it helpful to arrange a time in between the counselor's regular appointments for our child to drop in, meet the counselor, see the counseling room, and check out the toys. One counselor gave our daughter her business card and told her she could call with any questions. Of course, our daughter thought of several questions! At your child's first brief visit, schedule the first regular appointment.

You may even consider going with your child for the first appointment. We chose not to go with our daughter because we wanted to establish that she would be going to the counselor by herself. After asking for the counselor's suggestions, do what you feel is best for your child.

Be consistent with your child's appointments, especially during the first six weeks. The counselor and your child are getting to know one another, and your child is learning to trust. Learning to trust is a long and difficult process for a child who has been violated by an adult.

You do deserve a break, so you may want to choose a counselor who is willing to give you weeks off from appointments. Our daughter's first counselor only allowed for two weeks off during the summer while she was on vacation, which did not coincide with our planned vacation time. We found this situation frustrating and limiting. After much negotiation, she did allow our daughter to miss one week without paying for the session. It is always best to know the professional's policies ahead of time. Most counselors are willing to work with your family's calendar. After all, there is life outside of counseling!

Professional Assessment of Your Child

Most likely, you will be asked to fill out a lengthy inventory of your child's life beginning with conception (or adoption) through current development. You will be asked when the child did certain behaviors and how often and strongly he did these behaviors.

Observation techniques are one of the most valuable assessment techniques. Observations may be made at the counselor's office or at school. The parent may be asked to work or play with the child while the therapist observes.

Changing Counselors

Sometimes it may be necessary to change counselors, such as when you move or when you feel that a different counselor would be better for your child and family. Since we had no idea how to choose a counselor, we gladly used a referral for our daughter's first counselor. One year later, we were extremely frustrated. We never knew what was happening with our daughter in counseling.

One day I wrote in my journal, "We love her so much. I feel so heartbroken and scared, I feel like I don't know what's going on in therapy and how to react to what goes on at home. I feel so in the dark."

Two weeks later, I wrote, "We continue to feel frustrated. It's all beginning to affect our younger daughter also. We need help as a family, and our daughter's counselor only deals with her. We don't even have insight into her counseling."

Because our daughter had a difficult time bonding, we were afraid to make circumstances worse by additional changes. Six months later, we finally decided what we wanted in a counselor and set out to find a new one.

Yes, It's True: Now What?

After much prayer and a lot of phone calls, we found an excellent new counselor. We gradually transitioned our daughter by seeing her original counselor less often while at the same time beginning to see her new counselor. Looking back, I wished we'd changed sooner.

The healing process will take time and energy. My daughter's first counselor was a forty-five-minute drive each way from our home. I was often tired of driving and waiting in the counselor's office. I always planned things to do while I was waiting, like paying bills, writing a letter, doing stitchery, or running an errand to help the time go by faster.

My husband and I believed that once our daughter began counseling, she would get better quickly. I'm sorry to say that's not what happened. Her emotions and behaviors got worse before we began to see any improvement. Many tears of helplessness and frustration were shed over our unrealistic expectations.

Sometimes we would see rays of encouragement. After a few months with her second counselor, we began to see she wasn't as depressed and became more affectionate.

During this time, I often prayed a prayer similar to what I wrote one day in my journal. "Please heal our daughter quickly and restore her completely emotionally. Please return her spark and restore the years the locusts have eaten."

No one told us about the potential regression a child may experience before he improves. Our daughter regressed after therapy and cried like a baby. It was such a helpless cry. Sometimes after counseling she liked to be held and rocked like a baby which was nice, because she never wanted to be held much. I am happy to let you know our daughter did improve slowly over time. In the next chapter, we'll look at the grieving process that you're probably going through right now.

3

Since It's True, It Must Be My Fault

Hence these tears.
—Terence [Publius Terentius Afer],
Andria (The Lady of Andros)

March 8, 1989: After I shared about my daughter with a small group of friends, I felt like I had to get out of the room. I felt like I just wanted to cry. I guess I do OK when things are fairly stable, but I don't feel strong enough to handle ups and downs. (*Journal entry*)

May 9, 1989: I feel "emotionless" to some degree. I guess it's to protect myself from pain. My life feels like a monotone—no real ups or downs, highs or lows, just neutral for the most part. (*Journal entry*)

Finding out that your child or a child you love has been sexually abused is a shock. It produces grief similar to what one feels after a divorce or death of someone special. As I read through the pages of my four journals, I identified many emotions which are a part of the grieving process.

The five stages of the grieving process are: Denial, anger, bargaining, depression, and acceptance. During the grieving process, some of the other feelings I experienced were confusion, isolation, questioning, guilt, doubt, and hope. You may see yourself in some of these stages. I wish the recovery was as simple as going through one stage and moving on to the next.

What I found, though, was that the recovery process was more complex. One day I'd be angry, another day in denial, then another time accepting what happened. These feelings occur throughout the grieving process, but their intensity will fluctuate.

Stage 1: Denial/Shock

As parents and caring adults, we don't want to believe anything so horrible as sexual abuse has happened to a child. When we have undergone physical trauma, like a car accident, our body goes into shock to conserve energy and keep us off our feet. We become pale, have a rapid pulse and shallow breathing, and may even faint. When an emotional trauma occurs, we go into emotional shock, referred to as denial. Like shock, denial is a necessary response to bring back emotional health and should not be fought.[1]

Denial is a psychological defense mechanism that we use to protect ourselves. We screen out many unhappy or uncomfortable experiences or realities by ignoring them. In an effort to suppress a painful reality, we use denial as a largely unconscious mechanism to protect ourselves from anxiety and from hurtful reality. Matthew Linn says, "Through denial, I was swallowing not just the pain, but also the fear and anger...I also tried to swallow and repress my hurt feelings not with alcohol and drugs but with the more subtle escapes: work, TV, sleep and eating."[2] We come to the point where we don't feel anymore. We just feel numb.

In the denial stage, anxiety works like pain. Anxiety warns us that we are emotionally overloaded, especially with fear, anger, and guilt. If we don't think about the crisis, we hope that it will go away. We live in an instant fix-it society. We want immediate results now. People often suggest to those who are hurting, "Don't think about it. Just stay busy."

Their intentions are good but not beneficial to the healing process.

After we pass through the denial stage, the next stage in the grieving process is anger.

Stage 2: Anger

November 30, 1988: What did I do to deserve this? (*Journal entry*)

February 14, 1989: Once again, I feel angry at God for allowing my daughter to be abused. God, where were you? Why? You could have stopped it. Why does an innocent child have to suffer? (*Journal entry*)

Grief's anger is irrational, born of frustration and often acted out in rebellion. When we are hurting, we tend to blame others. Anger always needs a target and who better than someone else? Anger may be expressed outwardly as rage, or turned inward and experienced as depression. A variety of symptoms can signal the presence of hidden anger: depression, accident proneness, irritability, erratic sleep patterns, fatigue, excessive drinking or overeating, headaches, backaches, and many other physical complaints.

How we were taught to deal with the emotion of anger as children often determines our anger response as adults. As I was growing up, my father expressed his anger in explosive and destructive ways. I often remember being told, "If you keep crying, I'll give you something to cry about." Due to fear, I turned my anger inward and was often depressed.

In my husband's family, anger was viewed as sinful and wrong. Anger was not expressed. Seven months after we discovered about our daughter's abuse, my husband still hadn't expressed anger. I couldn't believe that he wasn't angry. His response was, "What good would it do?" Several weeks later he was volatile with the girls and short with me. When I talked to him about it, he said, "I'm afraid that if I express my anger, it will all come out wrong." I explained that he was already expressing anger in inappropriate ways. He wasn't coping well. He had gained ten pounds and was more tired and irritable.

Repressed anger is unhealthy and can destroy us. Anger can eat you up from the inside out if not appropriately expressed. If anger is swallowed long enough, the body may rebel with ulcers, asthma attacks, hypertension, hyperthyroidism, rheumatoid arthritis, colitis, neurodermatitis, migraine headaches, coronary disease, and mental illness. The symptoms of anger match perfectly the symptoms of Type A behavior responsible for heart attacks.

On the other hand, feeling anger is as healthy a reaction to being emotionally hurt as feeling pain is to being physically hurt. Feeling anger enables us to identify the hurt and heal the anger in a healthy way. Sometimes working through anger and guilt puts us in touch with new fears and anxieties. David A. Seamands, in his book, *Healing for Damaged Emotions,* states, "Express your anger, but be sure that it doesn't lead you into any form of bitterness, resentment, or hatred. Now the strange fact of the matter is that unless you and I learn proper ways of expressing and resolving anger, we will become resentful and bitter."[3]

There are many constructive ways to deal with anger. Some people find it helpful to divert their anger into work by chopping wood, scrubbing a floor, or getting even with a dirty wall. Tearing up an old phone book, hitting a pillow, swimming, or taking a walk can all be positive ways to release anger. Anger needs tension, so anything that drains away tension, whether a hot shower, a hard run, or a relaxed walk, will help to diminish anger.

Some of the ways I expressed my anger were pulling weeds, doing aerobics, hitting a pillow, and expressing my thoughts verbally while my husband listened patiently. I found it helpful to write my feelings in a journal. One day I wrote, "I feel he should have to suffer and pay severe consequences for what he's done. I wish his... would be cut off. I feel everyone should know what he's done. I feel he should pay for all medical and counseling expenses. I also feel he should be made to get help so no one else will be victimized. The truth should be revealed as well as consequences to go along with it."

I was angry at myself for not protecting my daughter. I was angry at God. At times I even felt abandoned by God. I'd been taught that Christians aren't supposed to be angry. If Christians do admit that they're angry, most dare not admit that they're angry at God. Anger is an appropriate reaction when a person hears about the incredibly sick things people do to innocent people. Jesus was always angry at sin. He loved the person but hated the sin.

You may be afraid that if you express anger to God, you'll be struck down by a bolt of lightning. There is nothing you can share out of the agonizing hurts of your soul that God has not heard. God already knows how we feel about Him and our circumstances; there's no use trying to hide it. God is big enough to handle our anger toward Him. He still loves us and welcomes us with open arms to tell Him just how we feel. He will never turn His back on us, no matter what we express to Him. I find great comfort in being able to express the depths of my emotions to a loving God.

Stage 3: Bargaining

The third stage of the grieving process is bargaining. Bargaining is primarily a mixture of anger and depression. This stage can often be identified by such statements as "I am willing to... only if you..." Bargaining is a common reaction to hurts other than death. The perpetrator was a criminal, and he was getting off scot-free. I wanted everyone to know what he did and I wanted him to pay for it. I wanted revenge. Most of us have wanted to get even with someone for some wrong done to us. If a child we care about has been wronged, these feelings can be very intense.

There is really no such thing as getting even. God's Word has a different answer to revenge, "Do not take revenge, . . . for it is written: 'It is mine to avenge; I will repay,' says the Lord" (Rom. 12:19, NIV). Yet I struggled with God's answer to revenge. I felt I could take care of the situation better than God could.

Stage 4: Depression/Guilt

I could have prevented it, if only. . . I had never left her.
I could have prevented it, if only. . . I had been more careful.
I could have prevented it, if only. . . I had known.
I could have prevented it, if only. . .

The dark cloud of depression is filled with the "If onlys. . ." and "I should haves. . ." You could probably complete the "if only" sentence at least twenty different ways. Guilty feelings are almost inevitable in the presence of loss. In some respects, a child's innocence and childhood have been lost.

As a parent, you feel you should have protected your child from harm. "Guilt comes from something we did or said that we wish that we had not done; or from something that we think we should have said or done that we didn't do."[4] I was plagued with a heavy load of guilt—because I hadn't remembered my own abuse, my daughter became a victim as well. "While a person may genuinely feel blameworthy, usually our self-blaming thoughts are unrealistic; we are overly harsh with ourselves."[5]

Dr. James Dobson, in his book, *Hide or Seek*, states,

Guilt can interfere with a healthy parent-child relationship in numerous ways. First it can take the joy out of parenthood, turning the entire responsibility into a painful chore. Secondly, guilt almost always affects the way a parent handles a child; . . . Thirdly, through some mystery of perception, a child can usually 'feel' hidden guilt in his parents.[6]

Throughout all of what I discovered about my daughter, I felt consumed with guilt. One day I made a list of everything I felt guilty about. I had an entire page of guilt feelings. Some of the items I wrote were: "I'm not a good enough mother because my daughter has so many problems." "It's my fault she has so many problems." "I can't meet the needs of my family." "I should have protected her from being abused." The list went on and on. Each item cried out, "Guilty, guilty."

I'm sure you can come up with your own list of guilt feelings. Dobson suggests, "Each item should then be assessed as follows: Is my guilt valid? Can I do anything about it? If so, how? If not, isn't it appropriate that I lay the matter to rest?"[7]

I discovered that only a few of the items on my list were truly from guilt that occurs when I've broken God's laws. Examine yourself and ask the Holy Spirit to reveal any areas which are your responsibility. Quit making excuses for yourself or others and take responsibility for any wrong attitudes or actions you have. If possible, begin to right any wrongs. You may need to apologize to your child and ask for forgiveness. Don't beat yourself up over your mistakes, because we all make them. Make a choice to set things right with God and others and move on with your life.

If you're like me, you may have many items on your guilty list that are termed "false guilt." "False guilt erupts when we or others set up unattainable or superficial expectations of ourselves that even our Lord would not have attempted."[8] I did not prevent the abuse from happening, but once I knew about it, I got our daughter all the medical and emotional help I could find. In one journal entry I quoted from the book, *The Missing*

Piece. "The secret things belong to the Lord our God, but the things revealed belong to us." I had to focus on what I did do and not on what I could have or should have done.

I felt it was time to do something that I really wanted to do, yet I felt like our family was in such a mess that I needed to get it in order first. I felt guilty about wanting to do something for myself. I had waited ten years to return to college and earn my master's degree. I was registered to begin school, but I began to feel guilty about going back to college. I also knew it was healthy for me to have time away.

Guilt causes a loss of self-respect and feelings of deserving condemnation for sin. Romans 8:1 says, "There is therefore now no condemnation for those who are in Christ Jesus" (NASB). I claimed this verse for each item on my list. I am learning to rebuke Satan when he plagues me with guilt because of my performance and not because of conviction of sin revealed by the Holy Spirit. I can't tell you how freeing it has been to be relieved of false guilt.

During the grieving process, I felt more and more tired until I had reached the point of exhaustion, yet I couldn't sleep at night. I kept getting sick. A simple cold would hang on for weeks. When I finally went to the doctor, he asked about my home life. When I briefly explained what we were dealing with in our family, he said, "You're in the fourth stage of recovery, which is depression."

Depression exhibits feelings of helplessness, hopelessness, and powerlessness. The person who is depressed and dejected has a miserable countenance. He looks troubled, worried, and unhappy, as if he is bearing the weight of the world on his shoulders. Before a person can deal with depression, he must acknowledge it. For a moment, I thought about what the doctor said, and I knew he was right. I hadn't even realized I was depressed. Looking back, I must say he was an excellent physician to diagnose depression during the first office visit.

When I am depressed, I enjoy having "pity parties." Anyone who will join me in feeling sorry for me is welcome to attend. Self-pity seeks to make us feel good about feeling bad. We wallow in our misfortunes so they stroke and soothe us. Self-pity attracts attention to ourselves and demands stroking from others.

If the hurt is deep, it may take months to deal with depression and reach the final stage, acceptance. When depression is long term, involving suicidal thoughts or bringing major changes in patterns of sleep or appetite, then professional help is needed.

Stage 5: Acceptance

January 30, 1989: Lord, it hurts me so to see my daughter so emotionally ill. Please heal her. Restore her to the former condition of innocence, as if the sexual abuse had never happened. (*Journal entry*)

March 14, 1989: God is good. In spite of awful circumstances, I can still say, "God is good." My view of God is changing. (*Journal entry*)

June 23, 1989: It's not fair that my daughter should have to suffer lifelong consequences because of sexual abuse. But what counts is what will we do with our lives in spite of the fact that it's not fair. (*Journal entry*)

I finally realized that I couldn't choose my circumstances, but I could choose how I responded to those circumstances. I was heading towards the last stage of the grieving process, which is acceptance. A crisis is often a turning point in people's lives when they formulate new answers and priorities.

Denial and acceptance seem almost alike. In denial, people may smile, but their anger still gnaws away until they growl at themselves or feel God is unfair. In the acceptance stage, a person is free from denial and anger. A person experiences gratitude for growth from the hurt, an ability to grow from new hurts, an openness to feel all emotions, and a reaching out to others.[9] "As we profit from our pain, our sensitivity to others will increase. As we progress in our grief work, we can step outside our own pain to reach out to others."[10]

The way to wholeness is often through brokenness. When life as you want it to be breaks apart, only God can recreate it as He knows it should be. Brokenness is like searching for order among life's shattered pieces. I have seen God slowly put the pieces back together to make a beautiful stained-glass window. The reflection of Christ can be seen through the window.

I never realized how many hurting people surround me every day. Hurts and suffering are not exclusive; they embrace everyone and come in many different ways. Joni Eareckson Tada states in her book, *A Step Further,*

> Every person alive fits somewhere onto a scale of suffering that ranges from little to much. And it's true. Wherever we happen to be on that scale—that is, however much suffering we have to endure—there are always those below us who suffer less, and those above us who suffer more. The problem is we usually like to compare ourselves only with those who suffer less. That way we can pity ourselves and pretend we're at the top of the scale. But when we face reality and stand beside those who suffer more, our purple heart medals don't shine so brightly.[11]

I would never choose to go through this process again, and my heart is broken when I think about all my daughter has experienced, but God is healing my daughter and our entire family through the process. He continues to make stained-glass windows from broken pieces.

Temperaments and Grief

Marilyn Willett Heavilin explains in her book, *Roses in December,* four different personality temperaments.

She believes that each temperament responds uniquely to grief.

> The Choleric's major drive is for CONTROL. When Cholerics go through trauma, they try to deny the pain by becoming totally absorbed in their work, a hobby, or a social cause. They'll work furiously and may not want to come home for fear it will be too emotional and they might lose control.[12]

This was often how my husband would respond. He was so afraid of losing control that he worked longer hours than ever before. He couldn't seem to relax.

> Melancholies want PERFECTION. They want to be able to depend on how things are going to be; they're generally quite methodical. They will have medium highs but they have very low lows. A Melancholy trying to deal with grief may go into a deep depression.

I responded to the crisis by experiencing deep depression.

> Phlegmatics have a great desire for PEACE, sometimes peace at any price. . . .
> The Phlegmatic feels things very deeply but has difficulty showing emotion outwardly or expressing his feelings verbally. During an emotional crisis he may become extremely withdrawn and critical.

Our younger daughter responded to the crisis like a phlegmatic. She withdrew and spent more time alone. When asked what was wrong, she replied, "Nothing." It was difficult to get her to express her deeply felt emotions. We even spoke with her preschool teacher for ideas on ways to help her express anger.

> The Sanguine wants to have *fun*. . . . The Sanguine will continue to try to find fun even in the midst of his grief. He may display superficial joy and try to make people laugh. The Sanguine has a very strong denial system and will seldom let you see the pain that may be behind his happy face.

Understanding the temperaments and how each responds to grief will help you know how each family member may be feeling. As you can see from our family, each person's reactions were different.

Forgiveness

For those of us who believe in God, we often mistakenly expect all victims to be ready to offer instant forgiveness to those who have hurt them. On January 1, 1989, as I reflected on the past year, I wrote, "When will this ever end? It seems it goes on for years with new information being revealed and a continual struggle with forgiveness." I have forgiven the offender countless times, but the feelings of hate, anger, and revenge kept returning.

Counselors explained to me that I needed to experience the anger and pain first. Forgiveness was a process. I didn't want a process. I wanted to get on with my life. I wanted to forgive once and for all. Please understand that forgiveness does not mean we are releasing a person from responsibility for a crime or that we won't press charges or expect restitution.

S.I. McMillen, M.D. in his book, *None of These Diseases,* says,

> The moment I start hating a man, I become his slave. I can't work any more because he even controls my thoughts. My resentments produce too many stress hormones in my body and I become fatigued after only a few hours of work. The work I formerly enjoyed is now drudgery. . . . The man I hate hounds me wherever I go. I can't escape his tyrannical grasp on my mind. [13]

Lewis Smedes, in his book, *Forgive and Forget,* writes,

> Forgiveness is the only way to be fair to yourself. . . . Suppose you never forgive, suppose you feel the hurt each time your

memory lights on the people who did you wrong. And suppose you have the compulsion to think of them, (or your hurt) constantly. You have become a prisoner of your past pain. . . . The only way to heal the pain that will not heal itself is to forgive the person who hurt you.[14]

Forgiveness is a process that each person must work through in his own time. Lewis Smedes suggests that there are four stages of forgiveness. The first stage is hurt. When somebody causes you pain so deep and unfair that you cannot forget it, you are pushed into the first stage of the crisis of forgiving.

The second stage is hate. You cannot shake the memory of how much you were hurt and you cannot wish your enemy well. You sometimes want the person who hurt you to suffer as you are suffering.

The third stage is healing. You are given eyes to see the person who hurt you in a new light. Your memory is healed, you turn back the flow of pain and are free again.

The fourth stage is the coming together. You invite the person who hurt you back into your life. If he or she comes honestly, love can move you both toward a new and healed relationship. The fourth stage depends on the person you forgive as much as it depends on you; sometimes he doesn't come back and you have to be healed alone.[15] I prayed God would restore in me the love that was lost.

I continued to be angry that the perpetrator was walking around "scot-free." Why did my family have to suffer while he was going on with his life as if nothing had ever happened? In time, I finally realized he wasn't "scot-free." He was accountable to God, and a person isn't any more accountable than that. I made a list of all the revenge I wanted the perpetrator to experience. I released all the revenge I felt towards the perpetrator to God. Once I was able to release all the vengeance and let God take care of the results, then I was finally able to forgive. I felt so free. This time it really had worked. A new sense of calm came over me when I talked about what had happened.

Give yourself and your family time to work through the grieving process. Remember, it *is* a process. At times I would be extremely depressed and feel I wasn't making any progress. My brother suggested I look back six months or a year, instead of looking at the immediate circumstances. When I did that, I could definitely see healing. You, too, will see healing and progress over time.

4

Parents in Pain

We fell out, my wife and I,
Oh we fell out I know not why
And kissed again with tears.
—Alfred, Lord Tennyson, (*The Princess, pt. II, [song,*
As Through the Land, l. 4]

September 15, 1988: Lord, I feel so upset again. I know You are sovereign and yet I don't see the whole picture. I'm mostly struggling with the area of wisdom. We have sought You and asked for wisdom. We want the very best for our daughters and yet I feel like we've done so many things wrong. You promise us wisdom and I feel we've lacked wisdom in many decisions. (*Journal entry*)

June 30, 1989: Today was one of the worst days I've had in awhile. My self-worth is on the line. I feel lousy about being a mother. My ideals are so far from reality. I envisioned so much more as a mother, (including fulfillment and happiness). I never realized it would be so hard and discouraging. (*Journal entry*)

February 20, 1991: My sister's new baby is so perfect. How refreshing to be with a new mom and dad who have nothing but high hopes and dreams for their child. What happens to cause a parent to get to the point where we are when we sometimes wished our child lived somewhere else? I remember so well the pride and joy that radiated from us over our girls. (*Journal entry*)

June 1991: Ten years ago our special daughter was born. Many dreams have been shattered, but there are many previous memories. (*Journal entry*)

Dreams are shattered and sometimes die. Reality and the cruelty of life can set in. We don't know what each day holds for us and our children. My heart aches over what we've gone through. I wish it was different, but it's not. What will I choose to do with the broken pieces? God planned her life even before she was conceived.

Pick out any house and go inside. You can tell soon after entering if there are people just living there or a family. Even in the middle of winter without heat you can feel the warmth radiating from a family. Love, respect, understanding and thoughtfulness for each other are the links that bind a family together, but love is the strongest link of them all. Without love the others will soon snap.[1]

You are a parent in pain. You may or may not have the support and encouragement of your spouse. In fact, your spouse may be the perpetrator. Regardless of your situation, the crisis of your child's sexual abuse will affect your marriage. Recognizing that you and your spouse are in a crisis is helpful. One day I was thinking, *When will all these crises and events stop?* Then I realized they won't—it's called life. God can use every crisis to draw me closer to Him and teach me about His perfect love and grace.

When facing a crisis, it is a good idea to avoid making hasty major decisions. My entire family needed the stability of the familiar during our crisis. The increased stress of trauma can even have an impact on your family's health. The body's resistance is lowered and people can get sick more easily.

Unless unusual circumstances require it, this is not the time to move to a strange city, change jobs, buy a new home, or make other major decisions. Ordinarily, it is not the best time for deciding to have a child or to bring someone else into your family. Sameness and stability are important in working through a crisis. If at all possible, try to keep a daily routine.

Due to health problems, I had a hysterectomy at a young age. My husband and I wanted more children, so we pursued adopting a toddler or preschool child before we discovered our daughter's possible abuse. On the adoption application, we indicated we would be willing to adopt a child who had been physically or sexually abused.

When our daughter first entered counseling, we were advised to put the adoption on hold. When we discovered the sexual abuse and saw firsthand how difficult it was to raise a child who had been sexually abused, we realized that we did not have the physical or emotional strength to add a child with special needs to our home at that time.

After attempting to adopt for three years, the adoption was put on hold indefinitely. I still hope some day our daughter will be emotionally healthy and we will have the energy to add a child to our family. Putting the adoption on hold was an emotional and difficult decision for me. My husband was much more logical. I so much wanted another child that I tried to convince myself that I could handle an addition. It took time for me to realize that it would not be a healthy choice for our family. I had to accept the fact that I needed to concentrate on caring for the two precious children God had already given me. This was all part of the healing process.

Some people believe they can move on and grieve faster if they make changes in another part of their lives, thereby hoping to keep busy and diminish the pain of their loss. Actually, grief work is compounded and slowed tremendously when we start to cope with additional stresses or changes. Even positive changes will still have to be worked through.[2]

Try to include your family in what is happening and share

the feelings surrounding the event. Accept the help and support of others, remembering they would want our friendship and caring during their time of need. Try to be flexible about demands on yourself. If you or your spouse are perfectionists, this will be difficult for you. My husband and I are both "recovering perfectionists," so this was a challenge. It comes down to a choice about what is really important, standards of perfection or healing for your family.

Communication Is the Key

For many couples, a crisis pulls their families apart because the crisis will intensify nearly every aspect of marriage, good or bad. Although we'd experienced many difficulties, our marriage has been strengthened by this crisis. I'm excited to see what God will continue to teach us. Communication with your spouse is critical to the healing process for your family. Try to express your own feelings in a caring, nonburdening way. "When a husband and wife share a heartbreak, each must plot his or her own defense. You cannot plan the defense strategies of your partner nor can you plot a joint defense, for a heartbreak really is a solitary experience."[3]

If you had poor communication with your spouse before the crisis, communication won't improve automatically just because you are experiencing a crisis. If communication is an area you need to improve, I would suggest the book, *Communication: Key to Your Marriage* by H. Norman Wright (Ventura, Calif.: Regal Books, 1974). Good communication takes patience and work. Don't give up!

Majors and Minors

My husband and I found that we had limited energy and no reserves to deal with daily living. Every decision seemed to add more stress. What to buy at the grocery, the menu for the week, or how to spend our weekends became monumental decisions. Disciplining our daughters created tremendous stress. Even in counseling, our daughter's behavior got much worse before it got better. Basic survival became our goal. We just wanted to get through each day without major problems. We had to come up with a way to survive.

What worked for us was to "major on the majors," and "minor on the minors." As much as we wanted to deal with all the problem areas in our family, we had to choose what we called the "majors." We chose behavior areas we would enforce daily. Other "minor" areas we chose to ignore until the "majors" were under control.

Direct disobedience was a major area. What our daughters wanted to wear to school was a minor area. We tried to say "yes" as much as we could in smaller, less critical areas and focus on two to three major areas. You may want to list all the areas that you would like to change. Then rank the list in the order of importance to you and your spouse. Finally, key in on one to three of the top items on your list. When those areas are under control, choose other items from your list as new "major areas."

Handling Criticism from Others

Now, more than probably ever before, you need the support and loving encouragement from friends. I hope you are a part of a church family that will help you carry this tremendous burden. Unfortunately, many church members simply cannot believe abuse happens in Christian circles. Sometimes I found myself angry over hostile responses. At other times, I was so thankful for the help, support, and encouragement I received from people in the local church. Try to find a church where you and your child will be accepted just the way you are.

Parents are not usually prepared for the reactions of others to the news that their child has been sexually assaulted. I could write an entire book on the cruel things that have been said to my husband and me about our daughter and our parenting. Seeing others' shock and denial gives us a glance at our own initial feelings. Questions like, "Are you sure it happened?" or "Couldn't she be exaggerating?" hurt deeply. You may feel very alone and isolated. You will probably receive a lot of criticism, no matter what you do or say. You cannot control the fact that others will criticize you and your family, but you can choose how to best respond to the criticism.

When someone came up to me and said, "Do you know what your daughter did in Sunday School?" I would respond, "Is it positive?" "Well, not exactly, she..." I'd answer abruptly, "Well, I don't want to hear about it," and walk away. This response wasn't the best, but it was the only way I knew how to cope with the deep pain I was experiencing as a parent. I would walk away wounded, near tears. At times I envied parents who had "easy" children.

A counselor gave me some suggestions on how to respond more positively to criticism from others. I learned how to put some responsibility on them to help with the situation instead of carrying the burden all by myself.

One suggested response was, "Yes, God is helping my daughter with her challenge in life." I've acknowledged their comment and I understand she is a challenge. I can't imagine how they suspected that I didn't know about the problems in the first place, but some people enjoy being the bearer of bad news. Somehow it helps make them feel better about themselves and how they're doing as parents. We've all said it: "My child would never do..." We decide surely we are better parents than the problem child's parents.

Another good response is, "Thanks for what you're seeing in my child. I hope this will be an opportunity for you to pray for her," or "Thank you that you can have God's true love and be patient and kind with her." The response I liked the best was, "Isn't it wonderful how you can recognize the hurt in my child. Maybe you can help her." It might be helpful to take a few minutes and practice responding positively to the cruel comments of others.

Recently, we invited a couple for dessert. I had shared previously about my daughter's abuse with the wife. The day before they were to come I received a cancellation phone call. I told my husband the reason they gave me, but I said I knew that wasn't the real reason.

A week or so later, I discovered the real reason. She explained to me that they would like to get to know us better, but they didn't want their child to be alone with our daughter. She asked if I'd considered the possibility that she might do something to another child. I explained we were very aware of that possibility and outlined what we did to help prevent anything from happening. I asked her how she wanted to handle the situation, and we came to an agreement.

As I hung up the phone I explained the requests to my husband. I had mixed emotions about the situation. At first, I was angry and I wished I hadn't told her. I felt like the information was used against our daughter, yet I understood her concern. On the other hand, I realized it took tremendous courage for her to confront me with the issue directly. I wondered how many times others had pulled away or weren't willing to be friends because they didn't have the courage to discuss the situation honestly. I also knew we'd never become good friends unless I could share with her our hurts as well as our triumphs.

Over the years, we've had to separate our daughter from our adult friendships. One time, when a friend lovingly shared a situation concerning our daughter she said, "I don't want you to think this reflects negatively on our friendship." I explained that if I depended on my daughter for my friends, I wouldn't have many friends.

Sometimes my worst criticism didn't come from others but

from myself. I began to wonder if I'd made the wrong choice about being a mother-at-home. I thought when I looked back on the years I'd been at home, I'd feel good about them. Instead, I felt that since my daughter had so many problems and my younger daughter wasn't doing too well either, why didn't I just get a job and go to work? I believed that they may have been better off with someone else taking care of them.

One year, the day before Christmas I wrote, "My self-worth is on the rocks. I feel lousy and not very worthwhile. My daughter keeps sassing me and treats me like dirt lots of times. I was in tears over it. I'm tired of being treated like that. I asked my husband to help me. For seven-and-a-half years, I've tried to do special things for her and 98 percent of the time, she makes life miserable for me and everyone else. Then I wonder why I keep trying."

Another day, the Lord showed me that He didn't promise me perfect children if I stayed home. He simply asked for my obedience. I was obedient to His call to be at home. My husband would often remind me that we didn't really know the full impact of my being at home. He said that our daughter might have been even worse if I hadn't had the time to invest in her healing process.

Support Systems and Support Groups

Marriage, Family, and Child Counselor Bonnie Wilkinson, believes, "Support systems are so important because many of your traditional resources will disappear. Family and friends will sometimes not want to deal with the realities, a double betrayal!" Although many people will criticize and judge you, you will find special people who will come alongside of your hurt and be a help and encouragement.

Friends

Just the other day, I told my husband that we really needed "significant others" for our daughters. A "significant other" is someone who invests himself or herself in the life of a child by spending time and developing a caring, loving relationship, much like a special aunt or uncle.

As I was writing this section, the phone rang. On the other end of the line was a person calling to help our daughter in a unique way. She heard that we were struggling more than usual with our daughter and the Lord gave her an idea to help us. What she wanted to do was offer piano lessons free of charge for our daughter. She didn't want the lessons to add extra stress, but knew that our daughter had expressed an interest in piano lessons. The caller thought music might be soothing to my daughter, as well as give her one-on-one time with an adult. She would be receiving special attention, just like God was giving me special attention by answering my prayer.

You may find yourself withdrawing from your friends. Due to extra stress in your life, you may feel that you don't have the time or energy to invest in friendships. The reality is that you can't afford not to invest in your friendships. You need to be with other people.

When we're facing a crisis, we feel like we're the only ones who are hurting. We isolate ourselves and try to shut everyone else out of our lives. As we choose to spend time with others, we will have opportunities to be an encouragement to them. You will soon discover that the world is full of hurting people, not a whole lot different from you and me.

When my husband and I worked with the career singles group in our church, many of the singles were like aunts and uncles to our daughters. We have rarely lived near family since we've had children, so God has always provided an extended family of friends to fill that need. A single friend would call and take our children to the beach for the afternoon. Getting a ride in a convertible and a yogurt treat for their birthdays was a big hit. Sometimes a friend would take them to the mall or to McDonald's for lunch.

Not only were the singles significant to our daughters, but they were also a tremendous support and encouragement to my husband and me. Often one of the singles would baby-sit for us during counseling appointments so we wouldn't have to pay for a baby-sitter. A few of them helped pay for our daughter's counseling when it wasn't covered by insurance. We even had women who would care for our girls so we could get away for the week end. We will always be grateful to each person who has contributed to our healing process. I pray that God will provide special people in your life to help meet your special needs.

Support Groups

We were fortunate to have access to a support group for parents of children who learn differently. The program was sponsored by an evangelical church as an outreach to parents. Each month, a guest speaker addressed a different area of concern to the parents, such as Attention Deficit Disorder, dyslexia, home schooling, or gifted children.

We were always encouraged after attending the support group for two reasons. The first reason was that we didn't feel alone. We realized we weren't the only ones struggling in parenting a child with special needs. The second reason was that we were encouraged in our roles as parents. We weren't doing as poorly as parents as we thought. We had judged ourselves too harshly. The program also offered a support group once a month for parents to get together to ask questions and share creative parenting ideas with one another.

We have relocated since then, and we're looking for a new support group. We live in a much smaller community than Southern California, and currently there aren't any programs available. So we have to create our own group. We're in the process of finding other parents who are struggling with parenting and need support and encouragement. We're asking people we know for names of others who might be interested in a support group. Pastors and counselors are also excellent resources, as they often know of families who are dealing with problems.

You Deserve a Break!

You do deserve a break! Even though you are experiencing a crisis and you may not feel like it, you and your spouse need time by yourselves. So much of your time and energy is focused on your child and the healing process that it's easy to forget your responsibilities to your spouse. You *will* get through this crisis. Your child will grow up and move away from home. When the children are grown, it will be just you and your spouse alone again. The choices you make today will affect the rest of your married life. How you spend the years together raising your children will have a significant impact on your relationship during the empty-nest years.

If you are a single parent, it is even more important that you get a break. After all, you may have the entire parenting responsibility resting on your shoulders.

Whether you're married or single, you may worry that your child won't be able to handle your absence. You need to ask yourself, "Will I be able to handle my child if I don't get some time away?" I was a better wife and mother when I gave myself a break from parenting and the daily cares of life. You may be concerned your child will experience a crisis while you're away. I can't guarantee you that your child won't have a crisis during your absence, but you still deserve a break. You will have better coping skills and reserves to deal with the next crisis if you do get time away.

Also don't get so focused on your child that you stop doing anything you enjoy. I would encourage you to try and continue one weekly activity that's just for you. It can be anything, such as doing crafts, reading a book, going boating or fishing. If you don't currently have any outside hobbies, now would be a good time to begin something. You will need something to look forward to when times are tough.

False Accusations

Recent years have shown a growing number of false child sexual abuse accusations by one parent against the other to obtain sole custody, to terminate visitation or parental rights, or to harass a noncustodial parent. Sometimes the child accuses a parent or other adult. A growing number of false accusations coming from conflicting parental relationships are being documented, specifically when the custody of a child is in dispute.[4] Research shows that less than 4 percent of sexual abuse referrals involve a child making a false report of a sexual experience with a parent.[5]

If a child accuses a parent or other adult, the predominant view among clinicians is that the best course is to interview suspected victims by themselves. If the child will not be seen alone, a supportive adult can be with the child. When a child accuses a parent, some counselors suggest each member of the family, including any siblings, be interviewed separately. If their stories do not agree, each family member should be asked to comment on the lack of similarity.[6]

How will you know if the accusations are true? Indicators that the accusations are true include these situations:

1. The child has a difficult time disclosing or talking about the abuse.
2. The child makes several half-hearted retractions and subsequent reconfirmations of the abuse.

3. The disclosure is accompanied by depressed or anxious affect.
4. The child has difficulty confronting the alleged abuser.
5. The child is anxious or seductive in the alleged abuser's presence.
6. The child describes the sexual activity in age-appropriate language and can give a detailed description of the specific activities that took place.
7. If attempted or completed intercourse is alleged, the intensity of the sexual activity grew gradually over time.
8. The accusing parent is ambivalent about involving the child in the investigation.
9. The accusing parent indicates remorse for not recognizing previous signs of the abuse and for not sufficiently protecting the child.

Indicators that the accusation may be false include these situations:

1. The disclosure is made easily and is not accompanied by noticeable affect.
2. The child uses adult sexual language and is unable to provide specific descriptions of the sexual activity.
3. It appears easy for the child to confront the accused parent.
4. There is a discrepancy between the child's accusations and his or her comfort with the accused parent.
5. It appears the child is being prompted by the accusing parent.
6. Very intense incestuous sexual activity is described as beginning almost at once.
7. The parents are involved in a custody dispute or there are other signs of high levels of marital discord.

8. The accusing parent is eager for the child to testify at all costs and insists on being present when the child is interviewed.
9. The accusing parent gives only vague responses when asked about the development of his or her suspicion that abuse was occurring.
10. An older accusing child appears to be seeking revenge against a parent.

When Your Spouse Is the Perpetrator

When your child has been sexually abused by your spouse, your crisis is much more complicated. What are you to do? A child's home is to be a safe place, but your home is not. The sexual abuse must be stopped immediately. Don't think the abuse was an isolated experience. Most likely, it will happen again.

Studies show that approximately 67 percent of the cases continue for one to three years or longer. It is not just a negative slip of behavior that happens one night when the offender's defenses were down and out of control. The child is victimized over and over again with premeditated thought. It is an addiction of deviant and self-gratifying behavior.[7]

Mothers in incestuous families often resist recognizing and putting a stop to the incest. She may be afraid of confrontation, the perpetrator's violence, or losing her family. You may identify with some of these statements made by other mothers:

—"When my daughter started to tell me I just ran out the door. I didn't want to hear it."
—"When I first saw it, I wanted to kill myself. I prayed for God to help me."
—"I can't confront him on this, we haven't been married long enough."

—"I feel powerless to find a new house and make it on my own..."

—"I know he wouldn't abuse his own children."[8]

The discovery of the incest may mean you will have to live apart from your spouse until the molester gets help and is able to live safely with the child. The molester will have to leave the home, or you will have to leave with the child. A child should not continue to live with a perpetrator. Sometimes a noncustodial parent may sexually abuse the children during a visit. In this situation the abuse may be a way of getting back at the custodial parent.

At this point, you are probably terrified about your future. If you are a Christian, separation will go against your commitment to marriage. Listen carefully: I am not suggesting a divorce at this point. I am recommending separation until recovery is possible and the family can be reunited again. Some type of reunification occurs in approximately two-thirds of sexually abusing families.[9] As sad as this is for me to write, reconciliation is not always possible. The perpetrator may deny any wrongdoing and refuse to get help.

You may be consumed with fear and questions. Perhaps you have never had to live alone. How will you financially support your family? What will others think? As afraid as you may be right now, your fears do not justify your child living in an abusive situation. Your child deserves to be protected from further abuse.

Perhaps you feel paralyzed by the discovery of the abuse. You may have suspected the abuse, but found it so difficult to believe that you chose to ignore it. Now you are consumed with guilt. No matter what you did or did not do, you must now act on what you do know.

If you are a mother who discovered your own husband, or your child's father or stepfather, has sexually molested your child, you are in a triangular relationship. If you are in this situation, you may experience many doubts and questions. How can you ever trust your husband again? How can your marriage ever be the same again?

Your situation will be even more complicated if the perpetrator denies his involvement or blames the abuse on the "seductive" child. There are several excuses and explanations that are heard repeatedly.

—"I must have been drinking. I don't remember."
—"Penetration never took place."
—"I never knew she didn't want me to do it."
—"I did what any man would have done."
—"I couldn't help it. I'm in love with her."[10]

Mothers in incestuous situations generally fall into one of three categories:

1. *Passive/collusive mothers* who, by remaining passive about an incest situation, give silent consent; many of them have experienced child sexual abuse themselves.
2. *Unaware/unbelieving mothers* who cannot/will not believe the child's report, thus doing great damage to the child's trust as well as recovery potential.
3. *Shocked/grieved mothers* who are prepared to act on behalf of the child. These mothers give the child the best chance to recover.[11]

Sexual abuse is a symptom of a troubled family. Families in which sexual abuse is occurring may give the impression to the outside world that everything is fine. Everything is not fine. Sometimes the abuser may use this image of the happy family to coerce his victim into cooperating with his sexual demands. The victim is told by the abuser that he or she is helping to keep the family together. The truth is, sexual abuse does not occur in normal, happy families.

If you examine your own relationship with your spouse, you may find the relationship is poor. You may have no physical relationship and very little emotional contact. You may be strangers living under the same roof. Communication may be poor. In your home, perhaps no one talks with anyone in the family with any depth. You may think this is the way families are. I was raised in a dysfunctional family, but I didn't realize the dysfunction until I was an adult. It was the only family I knew, and I just thought that's the way all families lived.

You may wonder why a parent would turn to his daughter or son for sexual pleasure. This is not easy to answer. For some, the issue may be one of power or control. If an abuser considers his children to be his property, he has the power to do whatever he likes with them. The home may be the only place where he is in charge, so he exerts his power.

For others, sexual involvement with a child is the angriest act one can commit against the spouse. The major problem lies in the relationship between the husband and wife; the child is the victim.

Can Abusers Be Helped?

Yes, abusers can be helped. A perpetrator will need extensive counseling and support from others. Case studies show that successful completion of a treatment program is more likely in cases in which the legal system steps in and assists the family.[12] Please note, child sexual abusers do not become safe after only a few counseling sessions.[13] The road to recovery will be a long and difficult process.

Conclusion

By now, I hope you've realized you are not alone in parenting your sexually abused child. Keep searching until you find the support you need. There are many wonderful people who will come alongside of you and your family and help you on the road to recovery. No doubt you're looking forward to taking some much needed time away. When you return from your break, you can delve into the next chapter, "The Fragmented Family."

5

The Fragmented Family

Words that weep and tears that speak.
—Abraham Cowley (*The Prophet*)

As we have seen, the sexual abuse of your child affects your marriage. The sexual abuse of one child also affects any siblings and extended family. You may wonder how long will it take for your family to get back to normal. That is impossible to say. Perhaps the only predictability in your home is unpredictability. In our home, we didn't really know what "normal" was anymore, so we hoped for a "new normal."

Circumstances may never be the same in your family, but they may be better than they were when the abuse was going on. You may not see immediate progress, but if you look back six months or a year, you can usually see some progress and healing in your family. If incest was involved, the problems in your family have been there for a long time and will take time to be remedied. How willing are family members to work on the problems in your home? This will partly determine how long it will take to rebuild your family.

Talking to Children About Sex and Sexual Abuse

Many parents and adults suspect a child has been sexually abused, but they are afraid to talk with the child about it directly. Some are afraid of "putting ideas into the child's head." Some therapeutic stories have been written about incest, movies have been made, games have been invented— all in the effort to provide tools for talking with children about sexual abuse. Incest stories which have survived for centuries in myth and folklore provide metaphors about the incest experience. Stories can open up the topic of incest in simple and nonthreatening ways and communicate a variety of responses to the sexual abuse experience.

The child who has been sexually abused, as well as any siblings, need to be told in simple terms about what happened, why it happened, and where the family is going from here. You may also want to explain the possible reactions of other children and their families. This will help children understand the range of feelings that people experience and, at the same time, help them feel less isolated.

Many parents feel siblings don't need to know about the abuse. They may try to hide what's going on, but children are very perceptive. They will soon figure out that something is happening. Trips to the counselor come at regular intervals. Siblings notice that Jason or Jennifer is getting more attention. There is no substitute for complete honesty with the entire family. Incest thrives in secrecy. Healing requires honesty.

There are several ways that you may choose to inform siblings about the sexual abuse. You may want to discuss the circumstances with your child(ren) at a counseling session. That way, the counselor can help if you get confused or frustrated. I found children's stories to be very helpful. I read stories about sexual abuse to my daughters, then asked questions about the story, their experiences, and feelings.

You can choose now to begin open communication with your children. Talking about the incident(s) can help protect siblings from abuse. If you are willing to discuss the abuse, children will see they have the freedom to talk with you directly if anything ever happens to them. If you are not accustomed to discussing sex with your children, you will find this even more difficult, but it is not too late to begin now. There are many helpful resources available for parents in the area of sex education.[1]

Special Needs of Siblings

My husband and I will probably never know the full impact of the abuse on our daughter who was not abused. She was very angry with her family circumstances, yet she was holding all her feelings inside. She would withdraw and say that nothing was wrong. We decided it would be helpful for her to have counseling as well. For several months, she went to counseling every other week. Then she went when she felt like she needed to go. Even at seven years of age, she'd say, "I want to go to counseling."

Although one research study showed that the siblings of the victim were the most disturbed family members one year after the incest had been revealed, there is almost no mention in the literature of the concerns of the siblings in an incestuous family or of how they should be dealt with during the crisis-intervention process. Siblings may be just as confused as the mother about whether to support the victim or the perpetrator once the incest is revealed. Because the siblings are a potential source of support for the victim, an exploration of these feelings with the siblings may be beneficial to both them and the victim. The siblings may also need the opportunity to express their fears about the dissolution of the family and about their own safety and the reactions of their friends if the incest becomes public knowledge.[2]

Although we don't know the full extent of the effects on our younger daughter, we do know that her sister's abuse has taken a toll on her. Often she is terrified when her sister is screaming, having a temper tantrum, and threatening the family. She responds by screaming in fear and helplessness. When this happens in a family of two children and two parents, each parent can deal with one child. So she wouldn't have to listen to everything happening, one of us would take our younger daughter for a walk or to the backyard to play with her dog until the immediate crisis was over.

Sometimes, there are two adults available, but several children in the family, or there is only one adult available. You have to choose which child you will be with at the moment. The most important thing I do is make sure each child feels physically safe. The emotional damage has to be dealt with later. My husband and I try to comfort each child after the crisis, answer questions, and try to explain what has happened and why. Often we really don't know what's triggered the crisis.

Our younger daughter knows about her sister's situation, but her feelings of hate, resentment, and anger still exist. Even this morning she told her dad, "You love my sister more than me." We don't love one child more than the other, but that's how it's perceived by both our daughters. We continue to assure each of our love and, even more importantly, of God's perfect love for them.

We are not perfect parents. Sometimes we are frustrated because we try hard to be good parents and often fail. We apologize for wrong decisions, not handling a situation correctly, or losing our patience and yelling. We need God's guidance moment by moment. We know God can use even our mistakes to teach us and mold us into His image.

Family and Triad Counseling

Although your focus is on healing your sexually abused child, an effective treatment program includes counseling for both parents and siblings as well. A special concern was the impact of having my daughter and me in counseling at the same time. I knew I needed to deal with my own sexual abuse. On November 18, 1988, I wrote in my journal, "I'm scared to be in therapy at the same time as my daughter, and yet I don't want this to hang over my head for years until she's finished therapy. It sure is scary. Please continue to reveal truth in Your time." We decided I could help her better if I was emotionally healthy.

During this time, I found myself frustrated and floundering around. I chose to cut back on responsibilities outside the home and focus on our family. With both of us in counseling, many days were very stressful. Our family had to work harder than ever to be more understanding during this period when our counseling overlapped.

If incest is involved, group treatment and individual counseling for the perpetrator will be necessary. Treatment for the child is often most acceptable to the parents, and other treatment recommendations can spin off from the focus on the child's adjustment.

At first, family counseling may seem threatening, but when the parents can see specific goals, it will feel less threatening. Some goals may include: improving the marital relationship, improving the child's school performance, increasing communication skills, and/or a plan for discipline in the home. My husband and I found periodic sessions with our daughter's counselor very helpful. The counselor can best help your family when he has a broader picture of the entire family situation. You can also gain information on your child's progress and get ideas about things to do at home to help your child.

Another aspect of family counseling is called triad counseling. Triad counseling brings the mother, father, and victim together. Judith Cooney says,

> If the family is to function as a family again, this is a crucial step in reorganizing roles and responsibilities. In triad counseling

each family member participates in defining the roles of the other members. The victim, who has frequently been used as an adult substitute, has the opportunity to become a child again. The adults, who have abdicated their parental roles, reclaim them.[3]

When the three of us first met with the counselor, our daughter was very resentful that we were taking away time from *her* counselor. Now, after we've all met together, we allow her some time to meet by herself with her counselor, even if it's for fifteen to twenty minutes. This approach seems to help.

We found triad counseling worked well when our daughter was nine years old. For the first few sessions, she would just sit fuming and not say a word. Eventually she began to express herself and a few times even let herself cry. We tried triad counseling when she was younger, but it was mostly unsuccessful. When she was younger it was more effective for us to meet with her counselor separately.

Reunification

How do you know when, or if, it is possible for a family to be reunited? Some researchers have found that is it not possible to reunite families after incest has been stopped, either through placing the child or removing the offender, unless two conditions have been met. The mother must show that she is willing and able to protect her children, and both parents must admit the problem, sharing a desire to remedy it.[4]

Some families begin reuniting by going on outings. By going to the park, movies, or for ice cream, they are in neutral settings. As the meetings increase in length of time and frequency, there will come a time when the perpetrator comes to visit in the home. This can begin with a short visit and build up to dinner or an entire evening.

Telling Extended Family

Perhaps you are wondering how your extended family will treat you. Probably the best indication is your past experience with them. If you are not close to your siblings, parents, or in-laws, it is unlikely that this experience will automatically make you closer. If you and your mother barely speak to each other, it is likely that communication will be even more strained.

On the other hand, sometimes a crisis draws people closer together. That's what happened with one of my brothers, my mother, and myself. My mother has even helped pay for some of our daughter's counseling expenses.

You will have to decide *who* you want to tell and *what* you want to tell them about the abuse. We needed help and encouragement, and, with great fear and trepidation, we slowly began to disclose information. Family members will all have their own opinions about the situation. My brother directed a shelter for women, and I called and asked him some questions. He was very supportive and sent me some helpful information.

He would call once in awhile and see how we were doing. One night he called and asked many questions. Since that went well, we ventured to tell someone else.

The next people we told were my sister and her husband. She was crushed and cried, but she and her husband offered their support and help. I can remember many times when she sent a card of encouragement. I would frequently receive letters and phone calls. She knew nothing about the topic of sexual abuse, so she borrowed books from the library and a few I had. She was willing to educate herself. She and her husband have kept our girls several times so we could get away by ourselves. I can call her anytime I need to cry, need some encouragement, or just want to talk.

It's not likely that all of your extended family will be support-ive. One brother is very angry and bitter towards me. He wants nothing to do with me or my family. He doesn't believe anything ever happened.

Other family members had a difficult time dealing with our circumstances because of their own pain and denial. As much as I would have liked their support and help, I realized that I couldn't heal the whole world. I could only change myself and get help for my own family. A person cannot be helped until she makes the choice to deal with her own pain.

Holidays were stressful because we had to decide where to spend our time. I realized I couldn't make people accept what happened to my daughter and me, but I could choose who I'd be around. At times, I felt isolated and needed to be with people who would support and encourage me.

One family member decided he didn't want to be alone with our daughters out of fear that they'd make something up about him. Other family members believed if we'd just let our daughter stay up later at night, we wouldn't have had so many problems. Some believed we'd caused her problems because we made her go to counseling.

No doubt, you will probably receive a wide variety of responses from family members. Although there will be those who won't cooperate, I pray you will find some family members who are loving and will do whatever they can to aid in the healing process.

If the perpetrator is a family member, you will, no doubt, be unpopular for bringing the garbage out into the open. I confronted the perpetrator about my own abuse and told him I believed he had abused my daughter as well. He claimed that he didn't remember molesting me, and he certainly would have remembered if he'd molested my daughter. We told him we would only allow our children to see him if we were with them at all times.

After the confrontation, none of us saw the perpetrator for almost a year. For two years, my daughters only saw the perpetrator in public places while we were present. My daughters were always given a choice about seeing him. Sometimes they didn't want to be around him. No questions were asked. After two years, we began to visit at the perpetrator's home once in awhile.

Jan Frank believes a child should have no exposure to the perpetrator out of respect for the child. Keeping the child away from the perpetrator communicates to the child that you totally believe the child and what has happened. If the perpetrator denies the abuse, Frank believes the child is at higher risk for further abuse.

I believe telling the family and confronting the perpetrator gets the abuse out in the open. In our family, since everyone knows about the abuse, no one leaves children with the perpetrator. Yes, there have been hurt feelings and many awkward situations, but things are not nearly as difficult as before the family secret was revealed, when we felt we were the sole protectors of all the children. If you want more information on confronting the perpetrator, please read step VII - "Confront the Aggressor," in Jan Frank's book, *A Door of Hope*. (San Bernardino, Calif.: Here's Life Publishers, 1987.)

Often you will find that extended family members simply refuse to believe what has happened. This can be extremely harmful if they have children and the perpetrator is a family member. You have a responsibility to help protect other children from being sexually abused. After all, wouldn't you want someone to tell you so that your children could be protected? In fact, maybe you wouldn't be in this crisis right now if someone had told you.

Some family members may demand that you not seek or stop using legal and professional services because they feel you will destroy the family name or divide the family. A few of my family members objected to my decision to write a book. Many of your family members may be angry. People respond to bad news in different ways. Some may withdraw from you, take sides, or blame others.

After you disclose the abuse, a domino effect of blaming can occur. Soon family members are blaming one another for their own behavior. The parents are blamed, the sister is blamed, the grandmother is blamed, even the pets are blamed. It is useless to go around blaming everyone. The fact is the abuse has occurred and you now need their help, love, and support.

How Extended Family Can Help

First of all, your extended family can't help you unless you've communicated your situation to them. Don't expect them to be mind readers. You may want to express what you need from them and how you would like them to help you. It is never an imposition to ask for help, but be sure to give the person the freedom to say, "No."

As with most of society, your extended family will probably know little about sexual abuse. If they would like more information, you can suggest books they can read. Sometimes they may be too embarrassed to go to the library and check out books on this topic. If you have books on sexual abuse, you could loan them your copies. One family member was willing to be educated, but she didn't want anyone to see her at the bookstore or the library.

Your job as a parent is never easy. You have many difficult decisions to make. Decisions made today will affect the rest of your life. You may want to decide today to talk with your children about sex, begin telling your extended family about the sexual abuse, and possibly consider a plan for reunification. In the next chapter, we'll look at creative ways to help the preschool child, the school-age child, and the adolescent.

6

Creative Ways to Help Your Child

Those who sow in tears shall reap with joyful shouting.
(Ps. 126:5, NASB).

As a parent, I often felt hopeless and helpless. I wanted to do something to help my daughter. I wanted to be involved in her healing process. It was difficult for me to put her in counseling and let the counselor take care of her. Her first counselor allowed for little parental involvement. Her second counselor thought the whole family should be involved in the recovery, not just the child and the counselor. My husband and I felt much more comfortable with this philosophy.

Understanding your child's development as a preschooler, school-age child, or adolescent will add creativity in helping the child. You may find yourself needing that box of tissues less if you're actually busy *doing* something to help the child recover. In this chapter, we'll look at preventing child abuse, child development, and ways to help children at each stage of development. First, let's look at prevention.

Preventing Child Abuse

Why do you need information on the prevention of sexual abuse? First of all, you want to protect the child from further sexual abuse. Second, if there are siblings, you will want to educate them so that they will not become victims. It is possible to teach a child after sexual abuse has taken place, but it is a much longer process.

An old adage says, "An ounce of prevention is worth a pound of cure." This is certainly true in the prevention of child sexual abuse. Unfortunately, not all child sexual abuse crimes can be prevented. Parents do not have omnipotent power to protect their children from abuse, but they can help protect them from assault by giving them truthful information about sexual abuse.

Most parents tend to think their children are well supervised and able to avoid danger. They don't want to frighten children unnecessarily. The purpose of educating children, however, is not to frighten them, but to help them know how to handle a variety of situations.

You cannot always be with your children. Children spend many hours in school and participating in after-school activities. Many children are in day-care programs. Children need to be taught how to react in specific situations. Don't assume that your children are being educated in prevention at school. Although many schools have excellent prevention programs, it is your responsibility to make sure that your children are receiving the necessary education.

Prevention of sexual abuse is built on conveying the following ideas at an early age:

- Your body belongs to you.
- You have a right to say who touches you and how.
- If someone touches you in a way you don't like, in a way that makes you feel funny or uncomfortable inside, or in a way that you think is wrong, it's okay to say no.
- If the person doesn't stop, you say, 'I'm going to tell' and then you tell, no matter what.
- If you're asked to keep a secret, you say, 'No, I'm going to tell.'
- If you have a problem, keep talking about it until someone helps you.[1]

Children are taught to respect and obey adults. When an adult molests a child, the child is confused about the role of adults. Respecting adults in general, but not in specific situations, makes this a difficult concept to teach children. Children need to learn to say "no" when someone attempts to violate their privacy.

When our girls were young, we taught them their private parts were the parts of their bodies their swimsuits covered. Children also need specific examples to follow. For example, you can tell your son, "If someone touches your penis, you can say, 'Don't do that. I don't like it.'"

Games are a good way to teach children skills. One game that appeals to a young child is "What would you do if . . . ? and who would you tell?" Suggest different situations and ask what they would do. If the child doesn't know what to do, then make suggestions. A game lets you teach skills without adding to fears and anxieties the child may already have. Remember, a child's attention span is short, so don't try to teach everything in one day. Repetition is important for the child to absorb the concepts. As the child gets older, he will be able to comprehend more complex information.

Children also need to learn the difference between good secrets and bad secrets. A good secret would be a Christmas or birthday gift, or a plan for a surprise party. We want to warn children about keeping a "secret pact" with any adult. Most likely, if an adult does something that he wants kept a secret, then the action is wrong. Child molesters often threaten children that if they tell, bad things will happen to them or that no one will believe them.

As mentioned in the previous chapter, books can provide an open door to discussing the prevention of sexual abuse. Books such as *No More Secrets for Me* by Oralee Wachter and illustrated by Jane Aaron (Boston, Mass.: Little, Brown and Company, 1983) can open conversation on abusive situations children might face. Prevention books usually combine aspects of saying no, yelling for help, running away, and telling someone. Prevention books also emphasize a child's sense of self-worth. Storybooks can be very effective since children identify more easily with story characters.

As your children grow older, you need to continue warning them about the possibility of sexual abuse. The book *Safe, Strong, and Streetwise* by Helen Benedict gives several suggestions to help keep your teenager safer.

1. Discuss family rules openly. . . .
2. Tell your teen your primary concern is for his or her safety. . . .
3. Discuss what will happen if these rules are broken. . . .
4. Tell your teenager to call you anytime help is needed, with no fear of punishment. . . .
5. Tell your child that you never want him or her to feel unable to tell you about a frightening event due to fear of punishment. . . .
6. Explain that you'd rather be told about something like a sexual assault, even if it upsets you, than be kept in the dark. . . .
7. Encourage your son or daughter to take a self-defense class. . . .
8. Contact a Child Abuse Prevention Education group and arrange for a course to be taught in your community.[2]

Screening Baby-sitters and Day-Care Programs

Good sitters are difficult to find. The best way to find a reliable sitter is to ask friends for referrals. No matter who recommends your new sitter, do your own screening. Never leave your child with someone you are meeting for the first time. Arrange an interview ahead of time when you can spend thirty minutes or so talking with the sitter. During this time, watch to see how the sitter interacts with your children and how calm he or she remains. Some questions you may want to ask of a potential sitter are:

1. How old are you?
2. What experience or training have you had with children?
3. Ask some "What if..." questions.

When you leave your children with a sitter, always remember to:

1. Leave an address and phone number where you can be reached.
2. Leave name and telephone number of a relative or neighbor who will be home and can be called if you cannot be reached.
3. Leave telephone numbers of the poison control center, police, fire department, and an emergency number.

With the extensive media coverage of the MacMartin preschool sexual abuse case in California and others, day-care centers have been subject to reevaluation by parents and professionals in child care. You will want a clear understanding with your child's care giver as to appropriate disciplining techniques. You and the care giver should agree on how you are going to deal with certain situations. As you screen day care centers, you will want to:

1. Be on guard for inconsistency.
2. Be on guard for a caregiver who places unreasonable demands on a child.
3. Be on guard for a caregiver who belittles a toddler or uses sarcasm.
4. Be on guard for a caregiver who *does not* show any signs of physical affection such as hugs, lap-sitting for stories, or good-bye kisses.
5. Be on guard for a caregiver who takes little interest in a child's activities.
6. Be on guard for a caregiver who withholds praise.
7. Be on guard for a caregiver who uses excessive forms of

discipline or punishments; for example, locking a child in a dark closet.[3]

Developmental Needs

Different stages of your child's development lend themselves to different treatment and parenting methods. Knowledge of a child's developmental levels is helpful. As adults, we need to be reminded that children think differently.

Just as there are stages to a child's development, there are stages to recovery in abuse. For example, a three-year-old may be able to recite the ABC's. When he gets older, he learns to write each letter of the alphabet. Later, he learns to put the letters together to make words. He's learning developmentally.

The process is the same for sexually abused children. Children who were helped at a young age will still need to reopen the issues of sexual abuse as they enter puberty and deal with their own sexuality. Let's look at the treatment of the preschool child, the school-age child, and adolescents.

The Preschool Child

The preschooler will be able to:[4]

1. show what happened, using dolls or play materials
2. say who did it
3. tell if it hurt
4. tell what the person said

The preschooler will be unable to:

1. give a time or date when an event happened
2. give a complete narrative account of incident
3. understand implications of revealing sensitive information

Behaviors that may result from sexual abuse at this age:

1. regression, which may take the form of loss of toilet training, baby talk
2. night terrors, fears
3. clinging behavior
4. curiosity and outgoing behavior may be squelched
5. child may act out at an older age, due to the ability to suppress now.

Helping the Preschool Child at Home.—It is easier to repress traumatic events at this age than at any other. If the family is relatively emotionally healthy and responds appropriately and quickly to the discovery of the sexual abuse, the recovery prognosis for the child is hopeful. As with any age, the child needs lots of love and attention. The child may not act affectionately with you or others. Try not to take the rejection personally.

Our daughter didn't want to be held. We kept providing opportunities for affection. She always had the choice whether to respond or not. Sometimes we would make a game and say, "I need a thirty-second hug." Eventually, she became more affectionate. The need for touch is critical to a child's development. If he doesn't get affection while growing up, often he will find affection elsewhere as a sexually active teenager. (See ch. 8.)

You may feel hesitant to touch the child. One adult victimized as a small child said, "All of a sudden, they stopped kissing me or hugging me. When I tried to hug them, they were O.K., but I didn't want to take the initiative all the time. When I grew up, I asked my parents about it, and they told me they didn't want to scare me. But that is exactly what pushing me away did."[5]

It is not unusual for survivors of child sexual abuse who were not shown love to have difficulty showing it to their children.

One survivor said, "I wanted to love my child, but I didn't know how. To me, touching was something that hurt, like when my father beat me or when my grandfather sexually abused me. My mother rarely touched me in any way so I had no help from her. I didn't see touching as something I wanted to do to my child—at least not the kind that hurt—and that was the only kind I knew."[6]

Any way that you can build communication with the child will be helpful. Interacting with the child as you play with dolls, puzzles, puppets, clay, cut-and-paste craft projects, and listen to stories or music are fun ways to help your child. Outside activities may include bicycle riding and playing on jungle gym equipment or swings. Sand tray play is especially effective for abuse victims.

Helping the Preschool Child Through Counseling.—Play therapy may help the child express his feelings about the abuse and help resolve his anxiety. A therapist can determine whether or not the child has adequate abilities to cope with the effects of the abuse. Important aspects of therapy are to understand the child's fantasies concerning what happened and try to prevent delays or distortions of psychosexual development and the onset of later symptoms. Work with the family is usually directed toward helping them understand the child's behavior, know how to respond to him, and to help the parents with their own anxiety and guilt.

For all children, nurturance and protection are of critical importance. Often, these elements are absent or poorly provided for children who are sexually abused. Treatment often focuses on those needs first. For the little girl or boy who has learned to be seductive to get attention and affection, treatment may include teaching the child to obtain nurturing and attention in more appropriate ways.

Since our daughter's symptoms exhibited themselves at a young age, her God-given sexuality was triggered early, instead of at puberty. We've seen her act so seductively with men that she's caused them to move away from her. We've had to teach her what is appropriate behavior and what is not socially acceptable. Eventually, the child needs to understand the appropriate affection that parents and adults show children.

The School-age Child (6-11)

The school-age child will be able to:[7]

1. give a detailed account of what happened
2. may or may not use dolls or play materials to assist
3. say who did it
4. tell in general terms when incident happened (e.g.: when I was in the third grade, during daytime, near Christmas)
5. tell where incident happened
6. tell duration of abuse (e.g.: since I was four years old)
7. tell first and last times incident happened
8. understand some implications of revealing "the secret" . . .

The school age child will be unable to:

1. give exact dates
2. understand why he/she is not to blame
3. suppress the incident as readily as a younger child

Behaviors that may result from sexual abuse at this age:

1. bedwetting, thumb sucking or other forms of regression
2. early or late to school
3. tantrums
4. pseudo-adult behavior
5. marked interest in sex
6. changes in grades, other behaviors

Helping the School-Age Child at Home.—The majority of children who complain of sexual abuse are school-aged. As with the preschool child, the child will need lots of love and assurance. A school-age child has better language and reasoning skills, and you will be able to communicate more effectively. There are many activities you can do with children or encourage them to do on their own.

I helped my daughter start a journal. She'd seen me write in my journal many times, so it was familiar to her. Often I would say, "I'm going to write in my journal now. Would you like to write with me?" Sometimes I'd give her ideas for starting sentences. For example, "I remember these terrible things. . . . I want to understand. . . . Today I feel. . . . I am angry about, . . . or I want to. . . ." Sometimes I encouraged her to write poems about how she felt. Poetry can express inner turmoil. My daughter's journal is private. Under no circumstances do I read it.

A school-age or adolescent could also write an autobiography. An autobiography could include the following ideas:[8]

1. Your first memory of the molest.
2. How long it continued.
3. How the molester set it up.
4. What happened?
5. How you were threatened to keep the secret.
6. Who, if anyone, in your family knew?
7. How did you try to tell?
8. How you were stopped from telling.
9. Whether there was a most devastating time and what it was.
10. Whether the abuse became known and how each member reacted.
11. What the most emotionally painful part was.
12. What happened to your life after it stopped?

A child who has been sexually abused will often blame others for everything. He may have difficulty taking responsibility for himself and expressing his emotions. A counselor provided our daughter with a list of positive, or "feel good," words and negative, or "feed bad" words. Some of the positive words included: *accepted, affectionate, excited, happy, important, joyful,* and *loving. Angry, depressed, embarrassed, hurt, jealous, sad,* and *worried* were some of the negative words. She wrote each word on a 3 x 5-inch card. She used the cards to express her feelings.

The counselor also suggested hanging a small bulletin board on her bedroom door. When she was angry or upset, she could pin up the word that best described her feelings at the moment. Sometimes our daughter needed to be by herself. We always told her that when she was ready to talk, we'd be available.

For many sexually abused children who are intelligent and have adequate impulse control, school comes as a pleasant relief. For them, school can be a predictable, safe environment in which their abilities and strengths are realistically appreciated and rewarded. For other children, whose behavior is less acceptable or who are too preoccupied with the problems at home to be able to participate in learning, school seems to confirm their feelings of inadequacy and alienation. The need for treatment then becomes even more pressing.[9]

Helping the School-Age Child Through Counseling.—Successful therapy for the school-age child is characterized by the rapid transformation of the sexual trauma into fantasy play which can be translated into reality by the child when necessary. Children have the cognitive skills necessary to describe the sexual abuse but are resistant to doing so except in fantasy play.[10]

Counseling goals for the child will vary depending upon the child's symptoms. Feelings of vulnerability, specific fears or nonspecific anxiety, confusion, and distrust are likely to be present, and it takes time to relate these feelings to the event(s) that produced them.

Intense anger may be felt towards the parents, who in the

child's opinion, let him down. The anger, on the other hand, may be undirected. The child may feel bad, worthless, unloved or unlovable, or lack a positive self-image. These feelings may lead to confused, self-destructive, or aggressive behavior which needs to be understood, accepted, and counteracted by concern for the child's welfare by the therapist.

School-age children's problems commonly addressed in counseling are:

1. Trust-mistrust. Most sexually abused children have a real distrust of adults. It takes a long time before the child can forget that the perpetrator was friendly, interested, ready to play, and eager to keep secrets. Being able to maintain trust even through the termination of therapy may help the child seek help in the future.

2. Need for nurturance. This need is exhibited in desires for attention, food, and possessions. Sexually abused children need a time and place set aside just for them. They may react strongly to any intrusion upon their appointment times. At times our daughter would complain about going to counseling and yet she strongly objected to missing an appointment.

3. Poor self-esteem. Poor self-esteem can be related to parental attitudes which are critical and allow little self-approval and little indulgence in pleasure. The lack of pleasure often seems to be part of a chronic depression, similar to that of the parents. Our daughter had very poor self-esteem and chronic depression.

4. Poor ability to express emotions verbally and nonverbally. Sexually abused children often have difficulty discussing their anxieties, fears, and emotions.

5. Tendency to regress during therapy hours. This is more common in preschool children, but its presence in school-age children may indicate how many unresolved problems the child has left from earlier stages. We came to dread counseling day, and the day after, because our daughter's behavior was regressive, bizarre, and unpredictable.

6. Poor cognitive and problem-solving skills. Many sexually abused children have difficulty performing intellectual skills on demand.[11]

Sometimes peer-group counseling is effective with children between the ages of six and eighteen. The child's school may offer peer group counseling. The recognition that they're not as different as they thought can be reassuring. Younger children need to use the group to understand clearly that what happened to them should not have happened, and it was not their fault. At one time, we considered putting our daughter in peer-group counseling, but decided against it due to financial reasons.

The Adolescent

The adolescent will be able to:[12]

1. tell exactly what happened
2. say when, how, where, duration, etc.
3. understand all implications of revealing the secret
4. may or may not be a "good" witness

The adolescent will be unable to:

1. understand why this happened
2. forgive the mother, who is most often seen as contributing to what has happened

Behaviors that may result from sexual abuse at this age:

1. extreme loss of self-esteem
2. promiscuity
3. running away
4. moody, depressed, crying jags
5. poor school performance

6. drop out of school
7. drop friends of long standing
8. sudden change in values, etc.
9. overly compliant
10. too many responsibilities for age
11. will have very little free time for extracurricular activities
12. behavioral regression
13. drug and alcohol abuse

Understanding Sexually Abused Adolescents.—Some researchers have found that older children are more affected by abuse experiences. The adolescent victim of sexual abuse is often developmentally more mature; therefore, adults sometimes assume the adolescent is better able to cope with sexual abuse. As parents and caring adults we need to remember that the adolescent is also in the process of forming his sexual identity and very vulnerable in this aspect of development.

The mood swings of adolescence make great demands on the therapists, adults, and parents who may find the adolescent "fine" in the morning but attempting suicide later that evening.

Intense guilt, shame, social withdrawal, depression, and sometimes suicidal thoughts may be the results of sexual abuse in an adolescent. Fears of being permanently damaged physically, sexually "abnormal," or morally inferior can all be results of abuse for the teenager. Peer group approval is so important that for the teenager it is difficult to face public knowledge of his experience or to share it with anyone, even a trusted friend.

As responsible adults and parents, it is important for us to protect an adolescent's privacy in every way possible. This may not be easy if the offender is prosecuted or if you need family cooperation. I wrote this book under a pseudonym to protect our daughter from the effects of her peer's discovery of her abuse.

Many assaulted adolescent girls are afraid people will think they are "sluts" if they discover they've been raped. Many assaulted adolescent boys fear they will be labeled "cowards" or "unmanly." Girls may fear the assault will make them lesbians. Boys may fear that they will become gay because they were assaulted.[13]

Teenagers are in the process of becoming independent, and talking about sexual assault with their family is particularly difficult for them. Sometimes they fear the discovery of the abuse will be used against then. One teenager thought that if she told her parents they would never let her out of the house again.

Adolescents are commonly in conflict with their parents. "It is particularly difficult for them to give their parents information that may be used against them, or having to feel dependent on their parents again. Many times, in their effort to be 'adult' in handling their problems, they don't ask for help for fear that others will think they are being childlike."[14]

Suggestions for helping a teenager recover:[15]

1. Don't change the rules about when and where your child can go now. . . .
2. Don't keep treating your child as special or fragile. . . .
3. On the other hand, don't force your child to get back to normal immediately. . . .
4. If the victim is a boy, he'll need special reassurance. . . .
5. Expect your child to go through a difficult period. . . .
6. Reassure your teenager that his reactions are normal and happen to everyone after a sexual assault.
7. Don't drop the subject of the assault forever. . . .
8. If you are a father, don't withdraw from the family with the sense that sexual assault is a woman's problem. . . .
9. If your son or daughter is miserable at school, discuss what can be done about it.

The Parent-Teacher Team

In my daughter's early years of school, I found myself dreading the process of starting back to school. At the beginning of one school year I wrote in my journal, August 20, 1989—"I dread the first few weeks of school. Most mothers are thrilled their kids are back in school. For me, it means starting over with another teacher, getting called, and sent notes. It's so hard on me. I know I can't take responsibility for my daughter and yet the consequences affect our entire family."

Over the years, I have learned that teachers can be tremendous assets to the recovery of your child. Establishing open communication will ensure that you know how your child is coping with school. You may find it difficult to tell someone that you don't know your personal struggles at home. If you keep in mind that you want what's best for your child and so does your child's teacher, it may make this easier. In junior and senior high schools, the child has many different teachers; therefore, you may only talk with one or two of your child's favorite teachers.

Three to four weeks into the school year, I usually meet with my daughter's teacher. This gives the teacher several weeks to get to know her and draw his own conclusions. Teachers are very bright; they have usually figured out our daughter will require some extra attention without my telling them. What the teacher may not understand is my daughter's background.

An informed teacher can be alert to the child's needs in the classroom. It was emotionally very difficult for me to schedule an appointment with my daughter's teacher each fall, but the efforts always paid off in the long run. I tried to contact the teacher before the teacher had to contact me, which made it easier on my ego as a parent!

Each teacher's response will be different. The teacher may deny what you're saying. One example I remember specifically was the issue of masturbation. When I asked if my daughter had been masturbating in class, the teacher said she hadn't. The next time I saw her, she told me she'd noticed that my daughter was, in fact, masturbating on the corner of her desk, just like I mentioned. Her teacher just didn't realize what she was doing.

After identifying specific problems that I saw in my daughter, the teacher began to see the whole picture. Elementary teachers see your child six hours every day in a consistent and structured environment. Often students will say or do things in school that they wouldn't at home. The teacher's involvement can be a significant influence on your child's recovery.

One year, our daughter's teacher also had a sexually abused daughter. The teacher understood our child's behavior, the stress on our family, and counseling appointments. The principal of the school knew our family's circumstances. The teacher had mentioned her child's abuse briefly in her job interview. The principal obviously remembered and assigned our daughter to her class. It's always amazing to see how God cares specifically for each one of us, even in the seemingly small details of our lives.

One year our daughter's teacher was young, enthusiastic, positive, and cared deeply for her students. She set up a contract system with our daughter. Three identified behaviors were divided into three parts of each day, a.m., lunch, and p.m. She could earn a total of nine happy faces each day. If she earned eight out of nine happy faces a certain number of days, the teacher would take her out for yogurt or ice cream. Did that ever motivate our daughter!

Viewing your child's teacher as part of your team puts a positive outlook on the recovery process. The more people you can get on your recovery team, the easier your job will be.

Recovery from child sexual abuse is extremely complicated and time-consuming. It's not a simple five-step program. Over time, the child will become healthier. In the meantime, you have the opportunity (some would call it a challenge!) of living with your child. For me, that's the hardest part of all! How do you manage the molested child on a day-to-day basis? Let's look at some ideas in the next chapter.

7

Managing the Molested Child: Part I

... in the mist of tears.
—Francis Thompson *The Hound of Heaven*

December 28, 1990: I prayed, "Please give us wisdom as You gave Solomon who asked for wisdom. Lord, we need creativity. I feel like we've tried everything—rewards, grounding, time-outs, loss of privileges, going to bed earlier, no television or video games, spanking, and reasoning. How do we teach and mold a rebellious and angry child? Only YOU can heal and shape her." *(Journal entry)*

A week later, I wrote, "Right now, everyone is just trying to survive. No one is doing well emotionally. Our older daughter has taken a toll on *all* of us. Our younger daughter is moody and mopey. She's acting out."

Parenting is a difficult job. Being a parent can bring tremendous joy, but can also bring feelings of frustration, guilt, and inadequacy. Learning to parent is a process that takes time. Being the parent of a child with special needs can be even more challenging.

We all carry emotional baggage. Past events influence how we perceive present and the future. Children carry their baggage for a longer distance than adults, so it is important to pack the contents with care from the beginning. As concerned adults or parents, we can help children repack the garbage of the past so that they will have a lighter load to carry throughout the remainder of their lives.

Sad statistics indicate the impact of sexual abuse on children:

1. 70% of adolescent drug addicts are involved in some form of family sexual abuse,
2. 75% of adolescent prostitutes have been involved in incestuous relationships,
3. Sexual abuse has been identified as one of the three main reasons why children run away from home, and
4. 50% of the children in a reformatory in Maine and nearly all the children in a Chicago reformatory had been sexually molested prior to commitment. [1]

Raising a child who has been molested is a tremendous challenge. A wide variety of emotional, physical, and behavioral problems can develop. In this chapter and the next, we'll look at the day-to-day management of the molested child. You may refer to this chapter often as your child grows and changes. You will find some of the ideas helpful now. Other ideas may work later.

Different areas will need attention as your child grows. Today, she may be wetting the bed and exhibiting depression. Six months from now, you could be dealing with a completely different set of problems. My husband and I have been encouraged because children grow in stages. If we didn't like a particular stage, we took hope in knowing the stage would pass and a new one would come along. At least parenting is never stagnant!

Discipline

June 30, 1989: I get angry with myself when I don't keep on top of discipline. *(Journal entry.)*

My husband and I have determined the discipline guidelines for our girls, but we get tired of enforcing them. About every six weeks, the two of us have a pep talk. The six-week cycle goes something like this: Things are fairly under control, so we start to slack off from consistently enforcing discipline. Our daughter's behavior gets more out of control. Then we get tired. Because we're tired, it seems easier to let things slide.

There is always a price to pay. Instead of dealing with each situation as it arises, we let negative behaviors build until we get angry, yell, and/or handle the situation negatively. Hence, the six-week pep talk to encourage each other to be consistent. When behavior is out of control, it's usually because we haven't been effectively following through with our chosen discipline techniques.

In their book, *Unlocking the Secrets of Your Childhood Memories,* Dr. Kevin Leman and Randy Carlson believe there are four parenting traps:

1. The trap of being too harsh
2. The trap of demanding too much or too little
3. The trap of discouragement
4. The trap of all talk and no action[2]

How we were parented often determines how we parent our own children. I know I have said, "I'll never do what my parents did to me," yet sometimes I find myself doing exactly what they did. To avoid these parenting traps, Leman and Carlson have identified three steps.

1. Identify the potential parenting traps in your own memories.
2. Identify the potential parenting traps in your lifestyle.
3. Disarm your parent traps (the lies that may be part of your lifestyle) by replacing them with the truth.[3]

Some discipline methods that don't work are guilt, unspecific directions, lectures, threats, yelling, pleading, begging, and sarcasm. How do I know they don't work? Personal experience! I've tried them all without any success. One fact I've learned about parenting is that I need a wide variety of discipline tools and prayer to be an effective parent.

One discipline method that my husband and I use is called "time-out." This an effective method when a child hasn't done what he has been told to do or has a bad attitude. It also works well when siblings are fighting. If they are separated in a time-out, they cannot continue fighting.

In time-out, a parent isolates the child for a short time after the misbehavior. We found the bathroom makes a boring place for a child to have a time-out. However, if you have teenagers, time in the bathroom could be a privilege! We give them a specific length of time for the time-out. We usually set the timer in the kitchen and when it goes off, they know their time is up. Additional time can be added for violations during the time-out.

"Grandma's Law" works well to enforce various rules, routines, and responsibilities set up in your home. This nonconfrontive method derives its name from a legendary grandmother who told her grandchild, "First you eat your vegetables, then you can have some dessert." What Grandma's Law really means is that parents insist that their children do whatever has been asked or expected of them. Then, and only then, can the children do what they want.

When my children come home from school, they immediately want to go out and play. I simply state, "As soon as your chores are done, you can go outside." Since they want to play, their work is usually done quickly. If your child ignores your request and does what he wants to do, a time-out results.

The most effective discipline we have found for our children is to use natural consequences.

"Natural consequences" could be defined as what would normally happen with no adult intervention, and "logical consequences" as letting the punishment fit the crime. These are ways to deal with children who act irresponsibly or like to let the parent do the work for them. Using such consequences means that the parents will no longer cover for the children or protect them from the negative consequences of their behavior. ... Following natural and logical consequences works best when these irresponsible actions have become patterns of behavior, and thus the parents have opportunity to decide well beforehand how they will carry out the intended consequences.[4]

If your child forgets his homework assignment, he suffers the consequences of not turning in his work on time. If a library book is turned in late, he pays the fine. If he damages property, he pays to have it repaired. If he loses a needed item, he pays to replace it.

Withholding attention works best with small children who pester their parents for attention, sometimes by whining, pouting, or pretending to cry. If you consistently ignore these behaviors, you will usually see a dramatic decrease in their occurrence. When you first begin this practice, the child will use attention-getters even more frequently, thinking he will eventually wear you down and get his own way. Try to withstand this initial increase in annoying behavior by recognizing the child is testing this new discipline. If the child's behavior gets too frustrating, you can use a time-out.

We found taking away privileges or assigning extra chores to be helpful consequences for negative behavior. For example, if a child doesn't do his required chores on time, he can be given additional responsibilities. Grounding and loss of phone privileges have worked well with our daughters after they began elementary school. A social life is extremely important to them. If we remove these privileges, we have removed their lifeline to society.

In many homes, children know there are "Dad's rules" and "Mom's rules." Children play one parent against the other. If one parent doesn't give the desired response, they quickly try a different approach with the other parent. If the parents are divorced and remarried, children have more people to play against one another to get their own way.

I try to check with my girls to see if they've already asked their dad and what his response was. I am blessed to have a husband who teams up with me in parenting our children. We determine the general rules and consequences together in advance. For the most part, our girls know we share a united front, so their schemes are usually unsuccessful.

No matter what discipline methods you choose to use in your family, there are two key principles to remember. First, decide in advance what the consequences will be for certain behaviors. That way, no one is surprised. Children and teens know what will happen if they violate curfew or talk too long on the phone.

Second, be consistent in enforcing the rules. I know from personal experience this is very difficult, but I have discovered the long-term results pay off. Children need guidelines and clear directions. Many parents give up because they don't see results quickly. Months of consistency are needed to see results. It is important not to quit disciplining the child.

Fears and Perceptions of Reality

A child who has been sexually abused may have many legitimate fears due to his traumatic experiences. He may also try to cope by denying reality, a favorite method of escaping in our society. For example, denial is primarily responsible for the tremendous problem of alcohol and drug abuse in our country. Many young people use these substances for temporary escape. Another way to deny painful reality is through psychotic experience. "The psychotic individual merely pulls down a mental shade and creates his own dream world. (Psychosis has other causes, as well, involving emotional and/or biochemical difficulties.) He 'copes' with his problems by refusing to believe they are there."[5]

When we took our daughter for psychological testing because we thought she was schizophrenic, we were told she didn't perceive reality. Mentally, she would actually leave reality. She would say things like, "You're killing my baby." She would do and say things that wouldn't make any sense to anyone else. She would be in this fantasy land for up to forty-five minutes and have no memory of what had happened when she returned to reality.

Managing Fears and Perceptions of Reality

Try to allow the child to be afraid without belittling his fears. The fears are very real to him, even if they seem ridiculous to you. Continue to give the child opportunities to experience life in spite of his fears. You do not know when the child may cease to be fearful.

My husband and I kept reassuring our daughter in small ways. Because she was afraid of people in costumes, we never forced her to go near dressed-up characters or Santa Claus. Each Christmas, we gave her the opportunity to see Santa. If she chose not to see him, we didn't push her.

I will never forget the first year she decided to visit Santa. My husband and I stood in line with our girls, and my sister and brother-in-law. As our eight-year-old daughter climbed onto Santa's lap, she gave Santa a great big hug. We must have looked ridiculous as we stood watching with tears in our eyes. Those tears represented rejoicing and hope. We were rejoicing because of visible improvement. We had hoped that some day she would be emotionally healthy.

If the child is afraid of the water as our daughter was, a water adjustment swimming class may be helpful. We became aware of these types of classes *after* our daughter overcame her extreme fear of water. Had we known about these earlier, swimming lessons would have been much less traumatic for all of us.

We spent many hours in verbal reassurance and holding a very fearful child. We kept stating truth regarding the situation, because eventually we felt she would learn the truth. We tried not be make a big deal out of little things. Since our daughter was afraid of the dark, we decided to let her sleep with the hall light on. This was a minor issue in our family, not a major one. We trust by high school graduation, she'll be able to sleep in the dark! In fact, we focus on the future in many areas. It seems to help when our perspective is long-range instead of focusing on the immediate.

Dealing with her lack of perception with reality was one of the toughest behaviors we had to experience. We felt so helpless because nothing we said or did could reach her. It was as though she was in another world. When we tried to talk with her after the incident, she had no memory of the experience. Her counselor suggested we continue to provide reality for her by stating the truth. Often she would say, "You're yelling at me," when, in fact, no one was even talking loudly or raising her voice. We'd simply had to state the facts.

As she became more emotionally healthy, she left reality less frequently, and the experience was less severe. However, this process took two years in counseling. Sometimes her behavior is still bizarre, but at least she has a conscious memory of the incidents.

Anger

Anger is a common emotional response to sexual abuse. As a parent or caring adult, *you* feel angry about what people have done to innocent children, especially if the child is someone you know. Understanding why a victimized child may be full of anger and hostility is easy. The sexually abused child will often lash out at everyone.

Our daughter had been in counseling for almost a year. She'd improved, but she was still a walking time bomb. She was an angry and bitter little girl. It hurt me deeply to see her that way. She doesn't understand why she's angry. She doesn't understand why she doesn't fit in. She wants to grow-up fast because childhood is too painful for her.

The child may be angry at the perpetrator for what he did; at the mother or parents for not knowing; at brothers or sisters for not helping her; and herself for not stopping the abuse. The abused child feels cut off from everyone and more alone than ever.

In cases of incest, the child can be angry at the father or step father for the following reasons:[6]

- she may be angry because he makes her do things she hates to do and knows are wrong, then makes her keep it a secret,
- he doesn't care enough about her to let her be just his little girl,
- he doesn't respect her privacy and the safety of her own bedroom,
- he doesn't stop abusing her, even when it hurts and she's tried to make him stop, and/or
- he has made her be untruthful to her mother and other caring adults because he told her this must be their secret and she can't tell anyone.

The child may be angry at her mother because...

- the mother doesn't notice the molestation or that the child is hurting
- she believes her mother does know but isn't doing anything to protect her—as is sometimes the case (see ch. 4.)

- her father said he wasn't getting enough sex from her mother, so she has to have sex with him, and/or
- she feels her mother loves everyone else more than she loves her. After all, that's what her dad said.

The child is often angry at herself because...

- she feels responsible for bringing on the molestation by believing her father who told her she'd been seductive (or whatever reason he told her), and/or
- for enjoying the special attention, privileges, and perhaps even the closeness she has gained from the relationship.

The child may be angry at her brothers and sister because...

- they didn't help her. She doesn't know whether they knew or not, but she does know they were not there to help her when she needed them, and/or
- she believes the siblings are loved more by their mother. By telling her that her mother loves her sister or brother better, the father causes a separation between the children so he can more easily isolate his intended victim. (Donna Miller, *Mothers and Others Be Aware* (Burbank, Calif: Restauration Books, 1983, 1985), 113-15.)

Anger Management

Many of the constructive ideas in chapter 3, "Stage 2: Anger," will also be helpful for the child. How you as a caring adult or parent handle anger will model ways the child can handle his own anger.

Victims and siblings can be angry. Our younger daughter obviously became more and more angry, but she held in her feelings. Her preschool teacher suggested we provide an "angry box" for her. My daughter and I covered a box with her favorite color wrapping paper—purple. We stapled together a book using plain white paper and a construction paper cover. The book was titled "My Angry Book." We included crayons, chalk, and felt pens in her box. For safety reasons, we did not include scissors. When she felt angry, she could get her angry box and express her feelings through drawing. She knew her box was private—just for her. We never looked in her box. The angry box idea was simple and very effective.

Another anger management technique is journal writing which was explained in chapter 6. Writing an angry letter or a letter of confrontation may also be helpful for the older child.

We gave our daughters the freedom to express anger. When they're angry, they can spend time in their rooms to sort out their feelings and calm down. Children are no different from adults in this area. Trying to deal with a situation when you are angry is not helpful. Sometimes we all need time to cool off.

Several resources are available to help children and teens learn to cope with anger. Our girls enjoyed one series of coloring/activity books with stickers. Some examples are *When I Feel Angry, When I Feel Sad*, and *When I Feel Scared*. (Jane Hammond Wendt, Mario Noche illus.), and *When I Feel Sad: A Coloring—Activity Book with stickers, age 7-9* (Anderson, Ind.: Warner Press, 1986). *Caution: Contents Under Pressure —Learning How to Handle Anger* by Fran and Jill Sciacca (Colorado Springs, Col.: Nav Press, 1988), is an example of what's available for teenagers.

Depression in Children

We don't usually associate depression with the carefree years of childhood and adolescence. However, depression can invade at any age and rob life of joy and hope. Infants who are not touched or held may exhibit depressive symptoms. Many researchers believe this condition may even interrupt normal physical development. A depressed toddler might not talk or play, and children may be listless and feel poorly about themselves. Teen suicides have become common. Fortunately, there are ways to treat childhood and adolescent depression.

Dr. Archibald Hart believes,

> Depression is a symptom which warns us that we're getting into deep water. It is, I believe, designed by God as an emotional reaction to slow us down, to remove us from the race, to pull us back so we can take stock. I would even say that it is designed to drive us back to God in terms of trust and resources. It is a protective device which removes us from further stress and gives us time to recover.[7]

I like his explanation because it puts depression in a more positive realm.

Depression can range from a mild feeling of gloom to an incapacitating state. H. Norman Wright explains depression in his book *Crisis Counseling:*

> 1.) A person feels hopelessness, despair, sadness, and apathy. It is a feeling of overall gloom. A move toward depression is a move toward deadness and emptiness. Feelings change, and there may appear an air of sadness about the person.
>
> 2.) When a person is depressed he loses perspective. The way you perceive your life, your job, and your family is discolored when you are depressed. Depression is like a set of camera filters that focus upon the darker portions of life and take away the warmth, action and joy from the scene.[8]

Why do children become depressed? It could be caused by any of the following reasons: a physical defect or illness; malfunction of the endocrine gland; lack of affection; lack of positive feedback and encouragement for accomplishments; death of a parent; divorce, separation, or desertion by a parent; parental favor toward one sibling; poor relationship between a stepparent and stepchild; economic problems in the home; moving to a new home or school; or punishment by others.

As an adult, you may find it difficult to believe a child could possibly be depressed, but denying that the depression exists will not make the depression go away. Denial will only delay the healing process and prevent the child from getting the help he really needs and is crying out for.

Early in our daughter's counseling, we were told that she exhibited symptoms of childhood depression. We couldn't see what the professionals were talking about. From my own personal experiences with depression, she didn't appear to be depressed. She was active and seemed happy.

One day, I told her I felt depressed. She asked, "What's depression?" I explained that depression is feeling hopeless, like you don't want to live any more. I will never forget her response. "Mom, I feel like that every day." My seven-and-a-half-year-old daughter was most definitely depressed, and I hadn't been able to understand her depression. My husband and I were trying to attach adult symptoms to a child. Although some symptoms are the same, they are often exhibited differently in a child or adolescent.

We also discovered depression in a parent can have an effect on the children.

Any child with depressed parents is five times more likely to become depressed, but scientists do not know if the reason is genetic or related to the way the parents interact with their child. Probably it is both. Children can inherit a predisposition to depression, and their environment may place them at even greater risk.[9]

Childhood Depression

A child who is depressed:
- feels sadness mixed with anger, sometimes directed toward himself

- may consistently feel tired, lose his appetite, or have trouble sleeping; may be hyperactive or aggressive (masking depression)
- expresses anger in the form of rage or denies being angry altogether
- may not recall dreams and fantasizes infrequently
- may see herself as bad and worthless; is preoccupied with herself
- may be unresponsive to others or responds to pressure and urging
- is rarely able to enjoy pleasure.[10]

Adolescent Depression

In the book *Why Teens Are Killing Themselves, and What We Can Do About It,* the author suggests the following reasons for adolescent depression:[11]

1.) A significant loss
    a.) Loss of self-worth
    b.) A loss in family life
    c.) Loss of security
    d.) Loss of reputation
    e.) Loss of other love objects
2. Habitual negative thinking
3. Physical-genetic causes
4. Drugs and alcohol
5. Mental illness
6. Unrealistic expectations
7. Learned helplessness

Managing Depression

Aside from professional help, there are many things that a parent or concerned adult can do to help a child recover from depression. Hallmark has a wonderful line of cards designed for parents and caring adults to give to children called, "To

Kids with Love." A card of encouragement may spark a child's day and give a visual reminder of your love.

Continue to provide opportunities for your child to talk with you and with God. The child may reject these opportunities many times before he feels ready to share his feelings. Hang in there; don't give up. Continue to be available.

You may be tempted to criticize the child for being depressed. After all, being around a depressed person is no fun. Focus on the positive instead. Try and do something different with the child. Perhaps you could take him out for some frozen yogurt or a soft drink. When a person is feeling low, a change in the routine can be helpful. Even children can get into a rut. What do you find helpful when you're feeling down?

Provide plenty of opportunities for exercise. Depression feeds on inactivity. Physical exercise can help the mind as well as the body. Go for a walk or bike ride with the child. Exercise helps stimulate the endorphins in the brain and can significantly improve the child's mood. Activity may help improve your mood as well!

However, if you see several symptoms of depression, or the depression lasts longer than two weeks, you may want to schedule an appointment with the child's doctor. Depression can be physically triggered as well as emotionally based. Norepinephrine is a neurotransmitter in the brain which controls emotions such as depression or euphoria. Two other important neurotransmitters are serotonin and dopamine. When the norepinephrine decreases to a certain level, the depression becomes physical and biochemical (in addition to being emotional). At this point, antidepressants can be prescribed.

Antidepressants work in different ways. Some increase the norepinephrine (Norpramine). Others increase the serotonin (Elavil), and some increase both norepinephrine and serotonin (Tofranil, Aventyl).

The decision to have antidepressants prescribed for our daughter came after much struggle and prayer. After trying everything else with little improvement, we finally decided to try medication.

In just a few weeks, we were amazed how dramatically her mood had changed for the positive. With her depression more manageable, she had the emotional and physical energy to deal with other problem areas in her life.

A blood test can be administered periodically to check the levels of antidepressants in the child's system. I believe medication should only be used in conjunction with professional counseling. The root cause of the depression needs to be resolved or the depression will continue to return.

Suicide

Suicide is the third leading cause of death among young people. Listen to the alarming numbers:

> In the U.S., more than 5,000 youth between the ages of fifteen and twenty-four kill themselves annually. That's an average of one suicide every 104 minutes. Besides that, mental health experts estimate that between 500,000 and two million young people attempt suicide every year—as many as 5,500 suicides per day. . . .
>
> They kill themselves most often between three P.M. and midnight in their own homes by using guns and by hanging themselves. They do it, not because they want to die, but because they want the pain of living to go away. They think they have no other choice. Their suicide attempts are rightly called, "cries of help."[12]

What teens may not realize, especially in the depths of a depression, is that suicide is a permanent solution to a temporary problem.

Experts agree the number of youth suicides is actually considerably higher. Parents often hide the fact that their child either made a suicide attempt or did kill himself. Unless there is clear evidence, officials do not list a death as suicide.

Realizing that a child you love is suicidal is very disturbing. Several times our daughter would curl up on the floor in the bathroom, and cry out in a pathetic voice, "I just want to die, I just want to die." When I saw her like that, I couldn't imagine how people could think that nothing had happened to her.

Myths of Suicide

Myth 1: People who talk about suicide don't commit suicide.—About 80 percent of those who take their own lives have communicated their intention to someone prior to the suicide. Any threats or suggestions about suicide must be taken seriously.

Myth 2: Once a person is suicidal, he is suicidal forever. —This is untrue. Many who have thought of suicide or actually attempted suicide have discovered answers to their problems and are no longer suicidal.

Myth 3: Christians will not commit suicide.—Unfortunately, this is not true. Christians and non-Christians experience all types of physical and emotional disorders. Because many factors can cause a person to consider suicide, no one is exempt. (H. Norman Wright, *Crisis Counseling, Helping People in Crisis and Stress* (San Bernardino, Calif.: Here's Life Publishers, 1985), 100-101.)

Myth 4: Talking about suicide in front of a depressed person might give him suicidal ideas—Bringing up the subject may actually help the depressed person to talk about his feelings.

Myth 5: If someone wants to commit suicide, no one can do anything to prevent it.—This is not true. Most people who kill themselves want to live but do not see any other way out.

Myth 6: If improvement is made after a suicide attempt, there is no reason for further concern.—If a person doesn't get help, the second try may seem even easier. "Eighty percent of suicide victims attempted suicide at least once before. A repeated attempt often occurs about three months after what seems like a period of improvement."[13]

Warning Signs of Suicide[14]

- Dramatic changes in behavior
- Increased moodiness
- Specific suicide threats
- Withdrawal from normal activities
- Drug and alcohol abuse
- Unusual neglect of personal appearance
- Personality change
- Overwhelming sense of guilt or shame
- Shift in the quality of school performance
- Changes in social behavior
- Extreme fatigue
- Boredom
- Decreased appetite
- Giving away treasured items

Managing Suicidal Behavior

Anyone who is suicidal is crying out for help. Please don't ignore this cry. If you suspect your child or a child you know is suicidal, please don't back away. Many times communities offer a hot line for people contemplating suicide. You may want to call the hot line to inquire about local resources.

You can ask the child or adolescent questions like, "What are you thinking? Do you have a plan to commit suicide?" People are afraid if they ask questions, it will cause a person to go ahead with their plan. Holding a person accountable is one of the most helpful things you can do with someone who is suicidal. Ask him to commit to you that he will call you, day or night, if he's feeling suicidal. I usually ask a person to give me the names of three people he will call if he feels suicidal.

Keep means of suicide out of the house. If you have a gun, keep it somewhere else. If there are medications that could cause an overdose, keep them at someone else's house, even if you have to go get the medication every day.

Ages fourteen to sixteen are the peak ages for adolescent suicides. "Incest victims with behavior problems and disintegrating families who are between 14 and 16 should be asked about suicidal thoughts and plans. Such children should be followed at least until the first anniversary of the incest accusation."[15]

If you are a concerned adult who works with youth, *Why Teens Are Killing Themselves and What We Can Do About It* by Marion Duckworth (San Bernardino, Calif.: Here's Life Publishers, 1987) may be a valuable resource. The treatment of suicide can often be beyond our skills as a parent or caring adult so professional intervention may be necessary.

Running Away

One million children run away from home each year, and the average age is fifteen. Forty-seven percent of the runaways are girls, and the majority of runaways aren't even reported missing by their parents. More than half leave home because of child abuse, and one third are sexually abused (Parents United paper). Running away is a common choice of girls who are trying to get away from sexual abuse at home.

Dr. Sam Janus reports in *The Death of Innocence* that at least 75 percent of the runaways in our nation are escaping incestuous abuse, but many children and teens run away from one bad situation to another. Seventy-two percent of young prostitutes and children involved in pornography have had some experience with incest.

Runaways differ greatly in their commitment to leaving home permanently. While most runaways are gone for only a few days and tend to remain within a few miles of their own homes, some do make a real break with their families and immediate neighborhoods. These teenagers get more than just a fleeting glimpse of life on the street.

Three general categories of runaways have been determined in *Child Abuse, An American Epidemic.* The first category might be best described as those who have left their homes in search of glamour and adventure. The second group includes those who cannot remain at home because of their own severe emotional problems. The last category consists of those who run away to escape from abuse. We're concerned specifically about the second and third groups.

The group of runaways who suffer severe emotional problems may or may not have experienced abuse. This type of person may experience very severe depression, anxiety, or mood swings. He will have difficulty relating to others and may not always be in close touch with reality. His escape from home may be an unconscious attempt to escape from his own feelings of upheaval. He's running away to escape, but his troubled thoughts travel with him.

The third group of young people may have fled their homes to escape emotional, physical, or sexual abuse, but the results are the same. A young person has attempted to leave an unbearably painful situation. To them, life alone on the street is more desirable than remaining at home.

Managing Running Away

What does a parent or caring adult do when a child or teen runs away from home? Our daughter was three and a half years old the first time she ran away. She was angry, packed clothes in her Strawberry Shortcake suitcase, and rode off down the street on her tricycle. Although we knew that running away wasn't normal child development, we weren't sure what to do. People we talked to about the incident didn't really believe she was running away; however, this incident was the first of many attempts to run away from home. The pattern of running away began years before we suspected any emotional problems.

By the time she was seven years old, she'd been in counseling for eight months. We were advised to let her run away from home and allow her to assume the consequences. My husband and I discovered we didn't have the power to make her stay. We couldn't keep her from running away by locking her in our home. Only she could make the choice if she'd continue to live in our home or not.

Simply stated, we told her we loved her very much and would be very sad if she chose to run away. We couldn't make her live in our house if she were unhappy. The dangers and consequences of running away were clearly explained. If she ran away and missed a meal during her time away, she would go without a meal or meals.

The next time she ran away was very difficult for my husband and me. Dinnertime arrived. We didn't know how we'd handle the evening if she chose not to return for dinner. I suggested that we'd have to call a friend to come over for support and encouragement.

Tension filled the room. We stalled as long as our consciences would allow and finally worked up the courage to call her for dinner. We were praying that she'd be near enough to come home for dinner. To our relief, she arrived promptly. She inquired if we'd really let her go without a meal if she ran away. We told her lovingly but firmly, "yes."

Become familiar with runaway shelters in your area. Let children know what's available. Even though you don't want the child to run away, a shelter is safer than living on the streets.

I can't tell you how heartbroken and terrified we are when she leaves home. I don't know how we'd respond if something horrible happened to her. I do know we have been unsuccessful in making her live in our home. We chose to not let her control our lives and our home. We determine the guidelines. She makes the choice whether or not to live within those guidelines.

Basically, we used a TOUGHLOVE approach to discipline. TOUGHLOVE International is a nonprofit organization that coordinates and provides service and support to the worldwide network of self-help parent support groups. The support groups consist of families that are being torn apart by unacceptable adolescent behavior. If you are experiencing unacceptable behavior in your home and you've tried understanding, reasoning, active listening, and tender loving care with little or no results, you may want to consider a TOUGHLOVE support group.

Even though our daughter was not an adolescent, my husband and I did participate in a TOUGHLOVE group in our community. We were so desperate that we were willing to try anything. Although most of the parents had older children, we found comfort in knowing that we weren't the only ones with a difficult child. For more information, check your local phone book or contact: TOUGHLOVE International Service Center, P.O. Box 1069, Doylestown, PA 18901, (215) 348-7090.

Giving her the choice to run away has somehow taken the fuel out of her threats. She can no longer use running away to manipulate us. As I write, the original Strawberry Shortcake suitcase sits packed in her room. She packed the suitcase again last weekend, "Just in case I need it," she explained.

After we established these guidelines, she has seldom run away. In fact, it's been more than three years since the last time she ran away. How we've handled running away may seem harsh to you. You may want to get an opinion from a professional counselor as how to best handle running away as there are other options available.

Emancipation

An alternative for stable and mature teenagers who are able to care for themselves financially and emotionally is living independently outside the home. A minor can legally live away from home if he becomes emancipated. Once emancipated, the parents' rights as the young person's guardians are terminated, and the youth is then given the same legal status as any adult in our society. He is now fully responsible for himself and his actions.

Emancipation is not always easily attained. Please check the laws in the state where the teenager resides for specific details. The young person is required to be completely able to provide for himself and must have the approval of his parents or legal guardians. In many instances, the parents are reluctant to relinquish control over their offspring and successfully block this arrangement.

Remember young people who have been maltreated at home and who feel unable to come up with a viable alternative living arrangement may find that an oppressive home life is more than they can handle. When every other path seems blocked, they may decide to run away. We have to help them find those other paths.

8

Managing the Molested Child: Part II

The Lord God will wipe away tears from all faces
(Isa. 25:8, NASB)

Managing Bed-wetting

Bed-wetting is a common symptom of child sexual abuse. Our daughter was completely potty trained and dry at night by two and a half years of age. She began wetting the bed again almost every night at four and a half years of age. At the time, we had no idea why this behavior began. The pediatrician suggested that we not worry about it until she was six years old. If by age six this was still a problem, he suggested that we take her to a urologist.

At least five hundred changes of sheets later, we sought help from an urologist. The physician had her keep a chart for two weeks, writing down every time she went to the bathroom. Once a day she was to urinate in a measuring cup and record how many ounces she urinated.

At the end of two weeks, we were told she had a small bladder capacity. Several suggestions were given to increase her bladder capacity, like having her wait a little longer each day before she felt she had to urinate. We also borrowed an alarm system from someone in our church. The alarm system was more hassle than it was worth; however, a year later we tried a similar system with more success.

After trying all these suggestions, I continued to change sheets night after night. I was getting sick of waking up to laundry every morning. The bed-wetting had been going on for more than one and a half years already. My daughter was also beginning to feel worse about herself. We finally tried medication, which seemed to help for awhile. In the meantime, we moved to a new area and set out to find a new urologist.

The Lord provided the most wonderful urologist for our daughter. He was so positive with her. He communicated information in a clear and understandable way. He always spoke directly to her, as if I wasn't even there. Eventually, she went to see him by herself, with the nurse present, of course. He would say to her, "I find that really smart children have this problem. They're so busy thinking that they forget about the plumbing." Her eyes beaming, *Yeah, I'm smart!* she thought. He even did magic tricks for her at some of her visits. Going to see this physician was a really positive treat for our daughter.

I explained to the doctor how tired I was of changing sheets. He immediately asked me why she didn't change the sheets. I hadn't thought of her changing the sheets. He said it wasn't punishment, but one of her responsibilities in our home. To this day, she changes her sheets when they're wet, at least when she doesn't try to cover them up by making the bed over the wet sheets! I've chosen to wash and dry the sheets for her, but she would be capable of doing that part as well.

The new physician had her eliminate certain foods he believed contributed to bed-wetting. She was to eliminate all citrus products, all cola products, and spicy foods, such as pepperoni. He continued to monitor her medication for a year. He did tests to rule out any blockages in the ureters. At the end of a year, he did a cystoscopy, which is exploratory surgery done on an outpatient basis to rule out any further problems. No physical problems were discovered.

Looking back, my husband and I aren't sure that we should

have chosen surgery. At the time, we didn't know of any cause for her bed-wetting. The cystoscopy ruled out any physical reasons, so at least that wasn't a concern. It wasn't until later that we realized the possibility of sexual abuse.

Bed-wetting can be extremely frustrating to the family and the child. Being positive and not condemning will be helpful. Bed wetters are very sensitive to their problem. Other children ridicule and laugh at schoolage children who wet the bed. As our daughter began to trust others and told a few friends, she discovered others who also wet the bed.

Overnight parties were a real concern for all of us. We wanted her to attend all-night events, but didn't want her to be laughed at when she wet. We came up with an idea which worked well for overnight activities. We pinned a large plastic garbage bag and bath towel one third of the way down inside her sleeping bag. If she got into her sleeping bag carefully, no one ever knew it was there. We sent an extra night gown if she needed to change her clothes.

She took the sleeping bag to the slumber party in a large plastic garbage bag. That way, in the morning, she could put the wet sleeping bag in the plastic bag and no one ever knew. One time, a friend asked her why she put it in a plastic bag. She quickly answered, "My mom wants to wash it when I get home." That simple and truthful answer satisfied the child.

I'm sure you will come up with creative ways to handle your child's bed-wetting so he won't be left out of overnight activities. Being left out only further compounds the problems of feeling different and isolated.

Hyperactivity/Attention Deficit Disorder

Hyperactivity/Attention Deficit Disorder (H/ADD) is a biological, genetic, neurological disorder. This disorder is not caused by sexual abuse; however, many sexually abused children have H/ADD.

The hyperactive child is persistently overactive, distractible, impulsive, and excitable in the eyes of his parents and his teachers.[1] The characteristics of the hyperactive child can be divided into four principal categories: overactivity, distractibility, impulsiveness, and excitability.

Overactivity can be seen in the child's excess energy, his restlessness, fidgetiness, and never getting tired. The child moves more than other children and cannot turn his motor off. He has a passion for touching things, especially poking and touching other children. He never walks when he can run and never sits still when he can be moving around.

Distractibility is exhibited in his short attention span, especially in the performance of tasks. When teachers and parents give him directions, he tries to listen, but "tunes out" after the first two or three words. He often loses items, because he forgets where he put them.

At least eight of the following symptoms are required to meet the criteria for the presence of attention deficit disorder with hyperactivity.[2]

- Restless, fidgets with hands or feet, squirms in seat
- Has difficulty keeping in seat
- Easily distracted by extraneous stimuli
- Has difficulty awaiting turn in games or group activities
- Blurts out answers to questions before they have been completed
- Has difficulty following through on instructions
- Has trouble sustaining attention in play or tasks
- Shifts from one activity to another without completing the first
- Has difficulty playing quietly
- Talks excessively
- Often interrupts or intrudes in conversation or play
- Does not seem to listen to what is being said
- Often loses things necessary for school or home activities
- Engages in physically dangerous activities without considering possible consequences

Managing Hyperactivity/Attention Deficit Disorder

Many parents of Attention Deficit Disorder children feel tremendous guilt. Each day, a parent sets out to be more patient and calm, which may last all of ten minutes. Although I always loved my daughter, there were many days I did not like being with her. I resented other parents filling me in on what my child was doing. Ninety-nine times out of one hundred, the reports were negative.

I was tired of her teachers calling me at home, scheduling extra parent conferences, and sending home endless notes regarding her inappropriate behavior. After awhile, I'd just read the note and laugh. What was I supposed to do with her? I had tried every parenting skill I knew and was still failing.

I'd heard about ADD, but I really didn't think my daughter was hyperactive. When my daughter was seven years old, the Lord provided me with a friend whose son had ADD. My friend showed me a list similar to the symptoms listed above to see if my daughter had ADD. I answered yes to every statement except one. I scheduled an appointment with her son's pediatric neurologist.

Sometimes it can be difficult to find a doctor who has experience with ADD children. Ask friends if they know of any doctors who have expertise with ADD children. Call pediatricians and ask about their experiences with ADD children. If possible, find someone who works frequently with ADD children. Our daughter's current physician is retired and two afternoons a week he sees ADD children. I can't imagine why anyone would want to spend their retirement with ADD children, but I am truly thankful for him.

If you have medical insurance, check to see if ADD treatment is covered by your insurance policy. Our insurance wouldn't cover the expenses because ADD was considered psychological under our policy. Sometimes you can petition for payment because most physicians consider ADD to be physically based.

The diagnostic appointment included two appointments of two hours each. Prior to the appointment, we completed a lengthy questionnaire. A general physical was given, intelligence tests related to neurological development were administered, lab work was completed, and we were interviewed as parents.

Most of the testing was done with just our daughter; however, part of the testing was done with us in the room. We were basically in the room to provide an additional distraction. At this time, she was given paper, pencil, and simple oral instructions to follow. She started off very well, but within minutes, she was drawing whatever she felt like drawing, paying little attention to the instructions.

We originally thought life would be easier if we had our daughter tested and could get her help. We'd follow the doctor's recommendations and see improvement. At the end of all her testing, medication was recommended. Everyone we knew seemed to have an opinion about medication and what we should do. Overall, people were critical of using medication for ADD.

I finally started responding, "Would you like to live with her for a week?" It's easy to say what you would do if it's not your child. When you're the one who has to live with the child, your response may be totally different.

After hearing so many opinions, my husband and I kept getting more confused. I finally called a pharmacist friend to help me sort out the pros and cons of medication. We finally used her recommendation to try the medication for a month and see if there were any improvements. She explained complications that would indicate immediately if we should discontinue the medicine.

During the first three weeks, our daughter's behavior seemed worse instead of better. She was awake for hours at night and couldn't fall asleep. Then, at the end of three weeks, we saw dramatic improvement. She could actually sit still and focus on a task. Medication, along with continued counseling to learn appropriate behavior, ended up being an excellent decision for our daughter and our family.

Most doctors will monitor a child's medication every three months. Over the years, the doctors made a few changes in the amount and type of medication. Periodically, she was given "drug vacations." These drug vacations were extremely difficult for our family, but necessary for our child. Some medications can suppress growth. These "vacations" allow the child's body some time to catch up.

Remember: any time your child is on medication, complications could easily arise. Be sure to ask your doctor any questions you have. This is your child and you need to understand what is happening.

Probably the best treatment of ADD is what is called a multimodality treatment. This includes a combination of several treatments. Diet is important to monitor in an ADD child. Some children can be treated simply by eliminating all sugar from their diet. This is a good place to begin. We try to monitor the amount of sugar that our daughter consumes.

Many ADD children have a difficult time adapting to change or new situations. We spent a great deal of time explaining what the schedule for the week would be. We went over everything that was to happen each day in great detail. This was helpful but frustrating because life doesn't always happen the way you plan it. I always gave explanations with a disclaimer statement, "This is the plan, but sometimes things don't work out like we want them to and you will have to learn to flex."

Behavior modification programs are also helpful. The key is to reward small efforts. For instance, don't start out saying a child will earn an extra privilege if he does his school work for one week. Divide the desired behavior into small segments, like morning, afternoon, and evening. If he does the appropriate behavior two of the three segments, a small reward can be given. Charts are helpful and motivating to many children since they can see their progress. For example, when he earns a certain number of happy faces, he will be rewarded with frozen yogurt. Slowly add additional requirements for a reward.

We used a ticket system successfully. Our daughters could earn a ticket for appropriate behaviors, like riding in the car without fighting, getting ready for school on time, or having a good attitude. They could also lose tickets for inappropriate behavior. We made a list so they knew exactly what behaviors they could earn and lose tickets for.

Saturday was ticket redemption day. Each ticket was worth five cents. (Determine your ticket value based on your budget.) The tickets worked well, since our girls were motivated to earn and keep all their tickets.

Our daughter has benefited greatly from counseling. Medication alone would have been helpful, but would not have solved her inappropriate behaviors. We found a combination of diet, behavior modification, counseling, and medication to be the most beneficial for our daughter and family.

Dr. Richard Bardrick, head of Rapha's Children's Unit, suggests ten ways to reduce negative behaviors:[3]

1. Address impulsive behavior patiently and consistently.
2. Identify limits and consequences clearly.
3. Have a range, or schedule, of consequences.
4. Warn once when dealing with disobedience and follow through with consequences.
5. Apply consequences immediately.
6. Help the child to understand reasons for making certain choices.
7. Label and clarify actions and feelings.
8. Provide the opportunity for restitution and saving face.
9. Punish the behavior, not the person.
10. Intervene early when the child misbehaves.

If you are a friend of a family who has an ADD child or a youth pastor with ADD children in your ministry, you can be a tremendous help and encouragement to the child and family. A few extra moments spent with the child or parent in encouragement will go a long way. Believe me, parents of ADD children rarely receive desperately needed encouragement.

Eating Disorders

Eating disorders affect 20 percent of females between the ages of thirteen and forty. Food becomes a trap when it is used as a substitute for love, friendship, or success; or when it is used to cover up more serious emotional conflicts. Dr. Terence Sandbek refers to the eating disorders anorexia and bulimia as "The Deadly Diet."

> The Deadly Diet almost always starts off quite innocently as a normal diet. As the person takes off weight, she is praised and congratulated for having so much willpower. When the weight is taken off—and sometimes surprisingly quick—the person begins to think that maybe a few more pounds would be good insurance.[4]

Some child abuse victims know exactly what they are doing when they overeat, and they know why, but they don't want to stop. Some victims become anorexic or bulimic. Bulimia and anorexia seem to be the only way that they can control their own lives. In either eating disorder, the problem stems from low self-image and from being unable to deal with very serious problems.

Types of Eating Disorders

Compulsive eating is an uncontrolled consumption of large amounts of food not based on hunger. Compulsive eaters eat past the point of full stomachs and sometimes past the point of nausea.

In *bulimia*, binges of compulsive eating are combined with

extended fasting, vomiting, or the use of medicines to rid the body of food consumed. Bulimia is commonly referred to as the "binge and purge" syndrome.

Anorexia nervosa literally means a nervous condition producing loss of appetite. Anorexics are self-starvers who consciously choose to ignore their hunger and, consequently, can waste away as a result of starvation. The American Anorexia Nervosa Association defines anorexia as a "serious illness or deliberate self-starvation with profound psychiatric and physical components."[5]

The Warning Signs

Sometimes it is impossible to know for certain if someone you care about is suffering from a serious eating disorder. If several warning signs are present, you should get a professional diagnosis.

Bulimia

- food binges followed by vomiting, fasting, or use of laxatives, enemas, and/or diuretics
- inability to eat without purging
- fear of not being able to control eating
- constant fear of being fat although weight is within a 15-pound (7-kg) range of what is considered normal for your age and height
- irregular menstrual periods
- extreme tooth decay
- swollen salivary glands, body cramps, and dizziness
- significant weight changes[6]

Anorexia

- Dieting even when not overweight
- Feels fat, even when not overweight
- Engrossed with food, calories, nutrition, and/or cooking
- Denies hunger
- Strange food-related behaviors

- Complains of feeling bloated or nauseated when eating normal amounts of food
- Intermittent episodes of "binge-eating"
- Loss of menstrual period
- Uses laxatives and/or vomiting to control weight
- Leaves for the bathroom after meals to secretly vomit
- Excessive exercising; overly active
- Weighs frequently[7]

Managing Eating Disorders

Dieters all share the same problem. The common denominator is being out of control. "EATING IS NOT THE ISSUE! The issue is the lack of control in all areas: physiological, emotional, mental, and behavioral."[8] If your child or a child that you know has an eating disorder, she will probably require professional help.

Inappropriate Touching and Masturbation

Soon after the discovery of our daughter's abuse, we discovered she was fondling her sister in the bathtub and in their bedrooms. We immediately began having the girls take their baths separately.

Later, our younger daughter said, "She's touching my private parts in the bathtub." I mentioned they weren't taking baths together anymore. She informed me that her sister wasn't in the tub with her, but had put her foot in the tub and was touching her sister's private parts with it. We realized we had to monitor more closely what was going on at all times with our daughters and other children. We couldn't trust her behavior to be appropriate. The bedroom doors had to be kept open when children were playing together.

When we moved to a two-story home, it became even more difficult to monitor their activities. We never knew what she would do to her sister or other children. Often our younger daughter would come downstairs to report an incident.

Our daughter's counselor suggested using a nursery monitor. This fantastic idea worked well for our family. We borrowed a monitor from a friend. We put the monitor in our daughter's room and the receiver downstairs. If she turned off the monitor, we knew immediately. We could keep a close ear on what was going on at all times. If it got too quiet, then we knew it was time to check on them.

The topic of masturbation usually brings up much controversy, especially in Christian circles. Our daughter began masturbating at two years of age, which is not uncommon. We expected this to be a normal phase of child development that she would outgrow. Family members denied she was masturbating. Nine years later, masturbation is still a common practice for her.

When she was four years old, we asked our pastor for advice on handling her excessive masturbation. He suggested we tell her not to masturbate and spank her every time because of disobedience. My husband and I did not feel this was the right way to handle the issue. Excessive masturbation is not disobedience, it's a sign of disturbance. When we sought advice from our pastor, we knew nothing about the sexual abuse. We are so thankful that we didn't take his advice and punish her for something that was triggered because of what had been done to her.

For the most part, I didn't really struggle with her masturbation until she started masturbating on top of the cat and the rabbit. One day we were guests at a home and she laid down on a big fur rug and began to masturbate. After this incident, we decided to handle masturbation differently.

By this time, she was in counseling. Her counselor suggested we allow her to masturbate, but give her guidelines, such as only in her bedroom. We explained to our daughter that masturbation wasn't appropriate public behavior. When we would catch her we told her if she wanted to masturbate, she could go to her room. Eventually, she said, "I'm going to my room to hiccy-up" (her term for masturbation.)

Masturbation is common for children who have been sexually abused. Counselors explained as she felt better about herself, became emotionally healthy, and resolved the issues from the sexual abuse, her need to masturbate would decrease. We have found this to be true.

Sexuality, Promiscuity, and Prostitution

Children who have been victims of sexual abuse are often far more aware of sexual matters than most children their age, or they may possess sexual information for which the family cannot explain a source. Girls who have low self-esteem are often known to sleep around with anyone in an effort to prove to themselves they are lovable and worthwhile people.

> The adolescents who find it most difficult to accept a responsible approach to sexuality are those who as children have suffered sexual abuse. The tragic impact is the tendency of an abused child to repeat the cycle when he or she is older.[9]

The Search Institute Study showed that one in five of 8,165 young adolescents surveyed worry that "Someone might force me to do sexual things I don't want to do."[10] Because sexual abuse often triggers a child's God-given sexuality at an early age, promiscuity can be a problem.

Donna Miller, author of *Mothers and Others Be Aware*, shared that the repeated molestation of her daughter had taught her all the wrong ideas of loving and family roles. Her daughter did not learn to relate to men who were not emotionally immature and abusive. The boyfriends that she usually selected had an immature personality and were in need of mothering. Her daughter's psychotherapist said there was a danger that she might feel her present or future relationships are no improvement over those that she had when she was a child. She might conclude that a true love relationship is not possible for her because of her past molestation.[11]

Researchers have found that many women with a history of childhood sexual abuse suffer from a sense of low self-esteem as adults. These women often experience sexual difficulties in adulthood. Women who were sexually abused as children described themselves as frigid, and topics of a sexual nature didn't interest them. Their emotional reactions were often extremely intense, and they quickly turned away from any sexual subject.

Other women who were sexually abused as children had almost an opposite reaction. Instead of describing themselves as frigid, these women stated that they were promiscuous by their own standards. These women complained that as adults they experienced difficulty in maintaining long-term relationships with members of the opposite sex. Many felt compelled to have numerous sexual partners, and some said that they felt that the only way to win a man's love was to seduce him.[12]

Also it is not uncommon for the incest victim to come to believe that the only way to escape her intolerable situation is to find another powerful male figure. A great number of these girls become pregnant without benefit of marriage or tend to marry at an unusually early age. Often such girls see marriage as their ticket to freedom.

Managing Sexuality and Promiscuity

Please refer to the resources and ideas mentioned in chapter 5, "How to Talk with Children About Sex and Sexual Abuse."

Teen and Incest Pregnancies

A sad reality of sexual abuse is the frequency of incest pregnancy. Teenagers who have grown up in chaotic families where sex education takes the form of incest have difficulty in recognizing with confidence either the presence or absence of pregnancy. Some girls finally tell about sexual abuse because they fear that they are pregnant.

An adolescent who becomes pregnant by a father or stepfather tends to conceal or deny the pregnancy. She may also deny that the pregnancy is as a result of an incestuous relationship. Abortion is rarely sought, especially if the family is intensely patriarchal or excessively chaotic. In the majority of cases, someone other than the incest victim ultimately provides mothering to the baby.

It's not the child's fault that she is pregnant through an incestuous relationship. Through the depth of your emotions, you may want to blame the child for what happened, instead of placing the responsibility on the perpetrator. *The responsibility always belongs to the perpetrator.*

Managing Teen Pregnancy

An incest pregnancy can create conflicts that seem even more destructive to the family and individual stability than the incestuous relationship itself. Once pregnancy has occurred, several interventions may be needed. A careful examination of the baby should look for congenital defects, sensory deficits, and retardation. Care may need to be arranged so that the young mother can return to normal adolescent activities.

Parents of girls experiencing an incest pregnancy cannot predict their own reactions. When faced with a crisis, parents may react differently than they expect. Some parents approach the pregnancy as a problem to be solved together. Although it may be difficult, this approach is the most beneficial for everyone involved.

Teenagers facing a crisis pregnancy need a tremendous amount of love, support, and encouragement. The teen is now faced with having to make adult decisions. The girl did not choose incest and risk the possibility of pregnancy, yet she has to pay the price of a resulting pregnancy.

Sometimes a parent will choose to side with the perpetrator. Pregnant teenagers are often kicked out of their own homes. If you are a caring adult in this teen's life, then you will have a significant role to play. She may need a place to stay, maternity clothes, a listening ear, and counseling regarding her options. Bethany Christian Services provides free counseling for crisis pregnancies. They also offer complete adoptive services. For more information, call toll-free, 1-800-BETHANY.

For additional teen pregnancy resources, please refer to the bibliography.

As you move through the healing process, I trust that the Lord is continuing to wipe away your tears. In the next chapter, we'll look at some more positive aspects of caring for or parenting a sexually abused child.

9

Building Self-esteem, Trust, and Friendships

Time, with a gift of tears.
—Algeron Charles Swinburne, *Atalanta in Calydon*

Self-esteem

Each child is created with unique talents and abilities. These can be developed and used to help and serve both the child and others. Or they can be used for self alone, or perhaps not at all. Every time a child with low self-esteem denies these talents or says that he can't do something before he's tried, he's closing off some part of his life.

Many women with a childhood history of sexual abuse suffer from a sense of low self-esteem as adults. How does this happen? This low self-esteem can begin as a result of sexual abuse. Because of their poor self-concept, sexually abused children do not believe that they are worthy of a relationship which is reciprocal, caring, or deep.[1] Our daughter felt frustrated as she thought that she was the worst kid in her class.

Self-esteem is a commonly used term, but what exactly does it mean? It means the child feels good about herself. A child with good self-esteem is not swayed by a molester's enticement that he'll really like her if she lets him touch her. She likes herself. If he likes her, that's nice, but OK if he doesn't. She knows she doesn't need to perform in any way to get people to like her.

Self-esteem also means, "The child does have a basic trust in herself—she thinks of herself as a friend—someone who is nice to be around. With that core feeling, she is confident to explore, to grow, to succeed, and thereby to enhance further her self-concept. She does not believe new experiences are doomed to failure because she is basically no good."[2]

Victimized children feel like they're the only ones in their family or among friends who are going through the trauma of sexual abuse. They can feel extremely isolated because they feel different from their friends and family members. Sometimes they feel or even act "older" than other children the same age. Often they don't seem to fit in with the normal activities of their peers.

The formation of a child's self-concept is an ongoing process. The child does not decide suddenly at age six that she is a wonderful person and does not care about others who may have a different opinion. Dr. James Dobson believes, "A child's view of himself is a product of two important influences; (1) the quality of his home life; (2) his social experiences outside the family."[3]

He also states, "Children don't fit onto a 'to do' list very well." It takes times to listen and talk. "Yet these are the building blocks of self-esteem, held together with the mortar of love. They seldom materialize amid busy timetables. Instead, crowded lives produce fatigue—and fatigue produces irritability—and irritability produces indifference—and indifference can be interpreted by the child as a lack of genuine affection and personal worth."[4]

A low self-concept keeps a child from learning how to succeed and from respecting himself or even liking himself very much. Often a perpetrator manipulates the self-concept of the child victim. Many offenders choose a child who seems insecure and promise love and friendship if the child cooperates with him. How well the child likes himself will determine his vulnerability to the offender's promises.

Self-respect can lessen a child's vulnerability to sexual abuse. In fact, self-respect is just another way of saying, "I feel good about who I am." Dorothy Corkille Briggs, author of *Your Child's Self-esteem*, believes there are two main convictions on which self-respect is based: 1. I am lovable (I matter and have value because I exist). 2. I am worthwhile (I can handle myself and my environment with competence; I know that I have something to offer others.)[5]

Rebuilding Self-esteem

Positive self-esteem can help prevent childhood sexual abuse, but what if a child has already been sexually abused? How do you help rebuild a child's self-esteem? The rebuilding process may be one of the most difficult experiences in helping the child to recover. The child has lost a sense of himself. He now holds a distorted and wrong perception of himself. Out of that wrong belief come wrong actions.

The term "self-talk" has become popular. Self-talk is the belief system that influences the way that you think all day long. Dr. Kevin Leman and Randy Carlson state, "Most people speak along at the rate of 150 to 200 words per minute, but research suggests that you can talk privately to yourself by thinking at rates of up to 1,300 words per minute."[6] They believe self-talk works according to several basic principles:

1. Your thoughts create your emotions.
2. Your thoughts affect your behavior.
3. Your perceptions affect your thoughts.
4. You think irrationally.
5. You can gain control of your thoughts and change them.[7]

As a loving adult or parent, how do you use this information to help a child? Take every opportunity to reinforce the child's sense of self. Praise your child for big accomplishments—and small ones. "That's a beautiful picture. I'm going to put it on the refrigerator so everyone can enjoy it." "Your room is really clean. I know you worked hard."

Parents can influence how a child perceives himself. Yesterday, I heard a mother of a fifteen-month-old child say, "Do you know you're going to grow up to be a troublemaker?" Chances are, if the child hears that comment enough times, he will likely grow up to be a troublemaker. The words we say can make or break a child's self-esteem.

When I hear my daughters verbally slaughtering themselves, I can help them restate the truth. For example, if they say, "I'm so stupid," I can help them restate that their actions may have not been the best, but *they* are not stupid.

Verbally reinforcing positive actions helps build a child's self-esteem. Try to minimize negative verbal responses. Helping the child achieve a sense of mastery can add to an overall positive sense of self.

Creating individual space for the child can also help build self-esteem. You may want to provide the child with a special bulletin board where he can display his belongings. Sometimes it's difficult to allow a child the freedom to decorate and arrange his own room, but a bulletin board can be an expression of himself. My daughters choose all their own clothes. As my older daughter began to feel better about herself she chose more contemporary clothing styles.

Encourage the child to excel in one area, because finding an area that he can excel in can help compensate for his weaker areas. Let him become the very best that he can in something *he* enjoys, not something you want him to do because you didn't have the opportunity as a child. H. Norman Wright, author of *The Power of a Parent's Words*, states,

> God created you to be you, but He created your child to be the unique individual that he is. Don't require that your child grow up to be a perfect reflection of you (or opposite of you if you admire the opposite traits.) Challenge him to be the best that he

can be at who he is. If you adjust your expectations to match God's, your frustration with your children will be greatly reduced.[8]

Each fall we encourage our daughters to choose an extra-curricular activity for the school year. They agree to participate for the entire nine months, even if they decide several months into the year that they don't like the activity. We believe that this teaches them commitment and gives them a fair chance to decide if it's an activity that they'll enjoy. They've tried gymnastics, baton, ballet, piano, and soccer. Sometimes it helps to find different activities for each child so they don't feel like they're competing with each other.

Last spring our daughter decided she wanted to play soccer in the fall. This wasn't the type of activity she'd selected in the past, so we were a bit surprised. This fall she completed her first soccer season.

At one of her first games, I watched her with tears in my eyes. The tears weren't because she was doing well or because she was doing poorly, but simply because she was doing something new. This was a sign to me that she was feeling better about herself and confident enough to venture out and try something new.

Ideas to Build Self-esteem

One family had a "I like me because" night once a week.

Each member of the family thinks up something good about himself to share with all of us. It doesn't have to be a big item, but sometimes it is. Everybody has a turn, including Mom and Dad. It may not sound like much, but we think in a world where there is so much put-down it's good to decide where we are up on ourselves.[9]

One family that I know uses the concept that it takes three positive statements to balance one negative statement. When one of their boys verbally attacks another sibling, he must say three positive comments about the brother to him.

Another idea is to help the child make a list of what he likes about himself and a list of what he would like to change about himself. Then categorize each item into "Things about myself I can change" and "Things about myself I can't change." The child chooses one thing from his life of things he can change and lists some steps he can take toward change. Encourage the child to focus on the things that he does well and enjoys doing. As he focuses on what's good and special about himself, he will begin to like himself more.

A fun way to help ensure the identity of each child is to ask each child to design his own flag, and then sew the flag on canvas or fabric. The flag is flown in the front yard on the child's "special" days, including birthdays or when special achievements are earned.[10]

We also use a special person plate that says, "You're the Best," which we ordered through Discovery Toys. One day our daughter was chosen for a part in the school play, and she got out the plate for herself to use at dinner.

Trust

What is trust? The dictionary defines trust as a "Firm belief in the honesty, reliability, etc., of another; faith, confident expectation, hope." Trusting has been defined as "the willingness to risk beneficial harmful consequences by making oneself vulnerable to another person."[11] Trust can also mean having faith in yourself, knowing that you can and will do what you promise yourself. Trust is knowing that you can depend on God, yourself, and others. Once you feel that you really can believe in yourself, then you can begin to trust others. Many victims have a distorted view of God because they couldn't trust their own fathers. This is why trust and self-esteem are so closely tied together.

Children carry what they learn about trust into adult relationships. Trust is probably the most valued quality wounded by incest. Incest victims feel betrayed and have learned not to trust. One adult victim of child sexual abuse stated, "How can you trust when you know that around every turn there is a new betrayal? How can you love when your love is used for an adult's pleasure? How can you care about yourself when others see you as counting for no more than the several body parts they can use for their own gratification?"[13]

When such early developmental issues such as basic trust, autonomy, and object constancy have not been adequately resolved, recovery at any age can be a difficult. Trusting someone else requires self-disclosure, risk, and sharing yourself with another person. Trust is built through risk and confirmation. When someone appreciates your gesture, accepts your gift of yourself, and, hopefully, gives back a bit of himself, trust can be built. Trust is destroyed when risk meets betrayal, rejection, or ridicule.

A victim of sexual abuse needs to learn to trust herself so that she is stronger and capable of making good decisions, especially in the area of her own welfare. A female victim must be able to reject improper gestures and overtures from males. She must be able to say no to anyone who tries to sexually abuse her, which could include her father, brothers, uncles, cousins, and others. If she is strengthened in trusting herself, she won't be as likely to be victimized again.

Each person has the potential to trust and believe that others will not take advantage of her vulnerability. For victims of abuse, the ability to trust has often been weakened, but victims can rediscover the gift of trust.

Learning to Trust Again

How do caring adults and parents help a child build his ability to trust again? A daily routine and consistency can help a child begin to trust the safety of the environment. He will begin to test the environment for the limits of that safety. I know that routine is very important to my daughter. She feels more secure when we have a regular routine.

In our fast-paced society, I realize that it is difficult for families to establish routines, but a routine may be necessary for the child's recovery. Please don't feel guilty if every day does not go according to the plan. Circumstances may require a change in your routine. In the midst of trying to establish a routine, don't forget to allow yourself and your family the freedom of flexibility.

When someone offers friendship to a sexually abused child, it is difficult for the child to believe that the friend won't hurt him. When a victim of abuse faces a relationship that also implies mutual caring and maintaining each other's best interest, she may be cynical. How does she know this time will be different? Can she risk hurt and betrayal? Talking with the child or adolescent about trust can help you determine her thoughts about trusting others. You can ask whom does she trust; how does she show someone that she trusts them; how does she define trust; and what breaks trust between two people? These types of questions may open doors to further communication.

Learning to trust again is the central issue of every family member in an incestuous family. This first step is necessary for individuals, even if the family does not reconcile.

In the process of trusting again, the sexually abused girl needs to understand:

- she may have problems with authority, especially with male authority

- she may have difficulty in intimate relationships
- the difficulties probably stem from her inability to feel trust when trust is appropriate, and to protect herself when trust is not appropriate
- her problems can be related to her history of having been dominated and exploited by her father, and feeling neglected and abandoned by her mother.[14]

Donna Miller believes if family reconciliation takes place, the sexually abused daughter needs to see change in the perpetrator in order for her to learn to trust again. The perpetrator must tell her that he is responsible for the abuse; he must demonstrate that he has changed; and she must be convinced of some of these changes in his attitudes and behaviors. It will take healing and time for a perpetrator to admit his responsibility and begin to make positive life-long changes.[15]

Friendships

An abused child often lacks social skills that may come more naturally for other children. Friendship skills need to be developed just like other skills. "Mastering friendship is no snap. The strength and tensile of a deep relationship do not depend on 'no strain.' Difficulties and problems faced together can help us grow."[16]

Building friendships involves risk. In seeking friendships, we make ourselves vulnerable; people take chances when they share themselves with others. One who accepts us just as we are is indeed a friend. For a child who has been sexually abused, taking a risk to build a friendship is very difficult because trust has been violated. A child may need much encouragement to take a risk and initiate a friendship.

Although our daughter was very outgoing and could initiate friendships, she didn't know how to maintain friends. One

teacher explained that the children in her class identified her as
the kid to victimize.

For a long time, we tried to protect our daughter's self-image
by not saying anything negative about her inappropriate behavior. We finally realized that we weren't really protecting her
at all. Children can be incredibly cruel to children who don't fit
in, and we had a choice to make. We could teach our daughter
appropriate social skills in a loving way, or let her learn by the
cruel comments of others. Teaching her social skills was not an
easy task.

What if no one wants to be the child's friend? Being without
friends is not only painful for the child but for the parents and
adults who love him. You may consider helping a child develop an interest in a special activity. Then he could invite one
other person to join him in the activity.

My daughter wasn't usually invited to parties or to play at
other children's homes, so it meant that we had to do most of
the inviting. We would plan in advance when a child could
come over to play. The invitation was usually for no more than
two hours. That meant I had to free up my time to devote to
supervising their play. There were many other things I would
have rather done, but this was a critical need for our daughter.

I had to keep my eye on her at all times. I felt a responsibility
to keep the visiting child safe. I had to monitor the activities
and give continual supervision and guidance. By the end of
the designated play time, I was completely exhausted, swear-
ing to myself I'd never have a friend over for her again.

That night, we'd talk about things that went well and only
one negative situation. We would come up with ways that she
could handle the situation better next time. It's tempting to
discuss every inappropriate behavior you observed, but that
isn't your goal. Remember, your goal is to positively teach
appropriate social skills. This will take countless experiences
for the child to reach this goal.

There were many days that I wondered if she'd ever learn to

get along with others. I hoped that some day she'd get invited to parties and to friends' homes more often. Many tears have been shed over her lack of friends.

One of my daughter's best friends was her cat. When she got upset, she would often take her to her bedroom. We could hear her talking to her cat and telling the cat her problems. She would cry and hold her cat. Her cat provided great comfort and a listening ear. Pets can be extremely healing in the recovery process.

One year, we had an opportunity to move to a new community. I spent the summer before we moved teaching our girls about friendship. Each week we did activities and read stories that focused on one aspect of being a friend, like honesty, listening, and sharing. Our activities were based on the book, *Friends, A Handbook About Getting Along Together* (Cincinnati, Ohio: Standard Publishing).

We explained that the move would give her a chance to make a fresh start. No one would know her and she could essentially start over in the area of friendships. My husband and I were motivated to help her make a positive start. The move was extremely helpful for her. We didn't realize it then but, looking back, it also gave us a fresh start as parents. Hardly anyone knew about the problems we'd had parenting.

Over the years, her social skills have improved greatly. As she got older, she began to understand that if her behavior was appropriate, she could have friends over more often. We even worked our way up to having a friend spend the night! Who knows, someday we might even have a slumber party for a group of her friends! Now, that's positive thinking!

Training a child in appropriate social skills has been tremendous work, but the benefits are amazing. No one wants a child to grow up socially unacceptable. If you are an adult involved in the life of a child who exhibits inappropriate social skills, it's easy to brush the child off and hope he'll go away. The child is already being rejected by his peers. Will you reject him, too?

Tears are streaming down my face as I recall the countless cruel comments that have been made to my daughter or to me about her. A hurting child or teen needs your love and encouragement. Perhaps you could zero in on one area and be an encouragement to help to change a specific behavior. Your investment in time will pay off.

A school program originated by a psychologist has been effective in training adolescents in friendship skills, with special emphasis on learning how to reach out to the hurting and alienated youth in school.[17] Helping someone else by becoming involved in another person's life is necessary in learning how to be a real friend. A child of any age can learn to reach out to others and become a friend. Your child will learn sensitivity to others through the hurts that he has experienced.

As I was writing this chapter, my daughter came home from school and informed me that she decided not to take band this year because she wanted to be in the peer counseling training program at her school. My face beamed with pride. Yes, God was using her hurts to help others. "You will be a wonderful peer counselor. You've experienced so many things, and you know what it's like to hurt." I assured her she would do well in this area and praised her for wanting to be involved in the lives of others. I feel that God is going to use her to make an impact in the lives of other students.

A book that I found very helpful for my daughter, covering a wide variety of areas, was *Letters to My Little Sisters* (Ventura, Calif.: Regal Books, 1984). The book contains thirteen chapters, including ones on self-image, popularity, peer pressure, friends, modesty, dating, and parents. A workbook is also available (Annette Parrish and Rick Bundschuh, Gospel Light Publications, 1985.) The book is written for young adolescent girls, but I found many chapters appropriate for a preadolescent. My daughter would read the chapter in the book and complete the corresponding workbook chapter. Then the two of us would arrange a time to go over the material.

Building Self-Esteem, Trust, and Friendships

We've covered a wide variety of topics together in the first nine chapters and shed many tears through the recovery process. Perhaps one of the most difficult challenges is that of legal issues. In the following chapter, I'll address some of the most common legal questions.

10

The Law, Your Child, and You

"To remember for years—
To remember with tears!"
—William Allingham, *Four Ducks on a Pond*

Sexual assault is a crime no matter how old the victim or what his or her relationship to the offender. Before we get too involved in answering common questions about sexual abuse and the legal system, let me say that laws vary from state to state and even from one county to another. The legal definitions of child abuse and punishment of offenders also vary from state to state.

This chapter will give general information about the legal system. To get specific information about laws where you live, contact Child Protective Services in your state or a lawyer in your community.

Right now, your first priority is to protect the child as much as is legally possible. Perhaps you've just discovered your child's sexual abuse and turned to this chapter first. You may want to know how to protect your child legally and if you should take any legal action.

What Are My Child's Rights?

The Child Abuse Prevention and Treatment Act of 1974 was established to encourage reporting and investigative action on all forms of child abuse in the separate states. Most states have responded by setting up statewide programs. The laws set up the limits within which the local law enforcement agencies, such as the police department, child protective services, and juvenile and criminal courts, must operate. The interpretation of the laws always depends on the county agencies, and individual judges.

A child, or even a group of children, can be taken into protective custody by the police, but the courts must be notified in most jurisdictions within twenty-four hours. An extension of custody can be requested for two to three days until a preliminary hearing in juvenile and/or criminal court can be established. Under the "equal protection" clause of the Fourteenth Amendment, the rights of all family members can be considered by the court. The ultimate court decisions may be months away, but in the meantime, adequate protection is provided for the victim and the victim's family. This protection also includes the perpetrator in cases of parental incest.

One of the most shocking ways of finding out about child abuse is when someone, other than the parent(s), such as a teacher, counselor, or doctor, makes a report to the police. When this happens and the child is school aged, the child is picked up at school. The parents are called to come to the police station. Neither parent may know why the child is being held. It may come as a total shock to the mother if the charges are stated and an attempt is made to arrest the father at that time.[1]

A year had passed since we'd reported our suspicions of our daughter's sexual abuse to her counselor. I was not shocked when Child Protective Services (CPS) finally called to inform me that they had questioned my daughter at school. Since our youngest daughter was not school aged, the CPS worker needed to interview her in our home.

Later, the CPS worker explained the legal implications and programs available for assistance. In California, Victim's Witness is available in certain circumstances. If the perpetrator admits his abuse of our daughter, we could file a police report in the city in which the abuse occurred. Our daughter would then be eligible for this program, which covers counseling costs. Check your state to find out what programs are available for your child.

I had been expecting CPS to call after I made the report to the counselor. The counselor was in violation of the law by not reporting the information until a year later, when we requested our daughter's records for a new counselor. It's always best to file a report than to be sorry later. The safety of a child may be at stake.

Most states have laws similar to California's Law PC #11166, which makes reporting child abuse mandatory. This law requires that any person (such as a teacher, doctor, or social worker) with knowledge of—or reasonable suspicion of—child abuse or molestation must report the child's name, whereabouts, and extent of injury within thirty-six hours to the police or welfare department.

A 1982 decision in the California Supreme Court held that no health professional needs to tell anybody anything while a patient is being evaluated and a comprehensive diagnosis is being made. This includes the audio and/or videotaping of interviews with any person involved and the obtaining of needed X-rays or photographs. The patient's clinical records are protected from illegal seizure. The court affirmed the legal possibility of eventual use of any material obtained in the course of helping a young patient. This is within the evaluation and treatment permission granted to physicians and hospitals by either the parents, the police, or child protective service agencies. Interpretation of this California concept by other state courts should be considered in obtaining evidence.[2]

The Legal System

In the United States, any case of sexual abuse is heard in a civil court (either juvenile court or family court). The degree of proof needed in family court requires only "preponderance of evidence." The one exception to this occurs in cases where the "termination of parental rights" is sought by a child protective services department. In order for parental rights to be terminated, the United States Supreme Court (1982) requires "clear and convincing evidence." In the usual civil case, the needs of the victim and the family are considered; nobody is on trial. It is not necessary to identify one offender or prove anything beyond that "the child's environment is unsafe," which is a very broad category.[3]

A variety of different situations could determine which legal route you will take. The perpetrator will fall into one of the following categories:

1. A stranger
2. Neighbor/family friend
3. Relative outside the home (Such as a grandfather, uncle, or cousin.)
4. Relative inside the home (father, step-father, sibling)
5. Relative with visitation (father)

Stranger

If the molestation is by a stranger, it is much easier to handle, faster to report, and to press charges. After the initial police investigation, the case is usually assigned to detectives for further investigation. The information on the case is compared to similar cases in order to narrow down the number of possible suspects. Whether or not the offender is apprehended, this process is a very difficult one for the child and the family. It is often confusing and frustrating.[4]

Neighbor/Family Friend

In Ohio, a five-year-old girl told her mother about a kindly, elderly neighbor's behavior. By the time the case went to trial, three adults, who as children had been molested by the same neighbor, had come forth with their testimony. He plea bargained. Ohio has no victim-witness program, so the victim's family will continue to pay thousands of dollars for counseling.

This is just one example of sexual abuse by a neighbor. If the perpetrator is a neighbor or family friend, it is relatively easy to protect a child from further victimization. You simply must keep the child away from the perpetrator.

The next step is to file a police report. Be sure you get a police report number. This number is necessary for you to access state victim's-witness funds for counseling in the states where this program is available.

Reports can be filed as "unsubstantiated" if there is not enough evidence to press charges at this time. The report goes on file for future reference. Just because a report is "unsubstantiated" does not mean sexual abuse did not occur.

The police report goes to the district attorney's office. If there is enough evidence, the perpetrator will be charged with a misdemeanor or a felony. When the offender is known, there is either an immediate arrest or an immediate decision that there will be no arrest. Often the basis for these decisions is not explained to the child's family. The most common reason for not arresting an offender is the DA's assessment that the case cannot be won. This may be due to inconsistencies in the child's story or lack of corroboration.[5]

The case will enter criminal court if the police investigation determines that a criminal act has been committed and can be proved beyond a "reasonable doubt." The legal system includes several possible criminal hearings for the accused. The *arraignment* is the formal reading of the charges against the perpetrator. The arraignment is held within seventy-two judicial hours of the arrest if bail was not arranged and the accused perpetrator is still in custody. The *arraignment* could be months later if the accused has been successful at a stalling practice of extending the bail. At this hearing, it is decided if the accused should be detained or have his bail continued. He is advised of the charges, given an attorney, and his plea is taken.[6]

Sometimes before the arraignment, an offender who has a lawyer may consent to a prefiling agreement in which the defense and state attorney negotiate the plea and recommend a penalty. If an agreement is reached between the judge and attorneys, there will not be a trial and the child will not have to testify.

The next phase will be a plea-bargain offer. In either the plea-bargaining phase or trial, the perpetrator can be required to go through counseling as part of the sentencing, as well as assume financial responsibility for the costs of the victim's counseling. At this point, the perpetrator can accept the plea bargain or go to trial.

The mother of the victim may be encouraged by the probation officer to write a statement regarding the history of relationships and requests for sentencing. One mother I know wrote an eight-page letter. The list of requests for sentencing ran another eight pages. Ten appendixes documenting costs were also included.

In her letter, she included the rough road of recovery from the trauma of the abuse and the lifelong psychological consequences for her child. Symptoms of sexual abuse she identified in her daughter were listed and explained. She included patterns of behavior which the perpetrator possessed. She placed total responsibility on the perpetrator. A medical report which showed clear evidence was included. She concluded the letter requesting permission to speak at the sentencing.

I hope that the lists of symptoms and information throughout this book will be helpful in writing this type of letter. You will want to state facts, but also be sure to communicate your heartfelt hurts and desires.

If an agreement is worked out without a trial, it is presented to the judge for approval. The molested child's family might have an opportunity to approve or disapprove the agreements, depending on the policy in that jurisdiction.[7] If the accused pleaded guilty at the preliminary hearing, the case goes directly to sentencing. Otherwise, sentencing is determined following the trial.[8]

The second phase in the legal system is a *preliminary hearing*, held in Superior Court for felony charges. The preliminary hearing determines if there is enough evidence for a trial. This is mainly a prosecution hearing since the defense attorney does not present any evidence at this time. If the charges are at a misdemeanor level, the hearings are held in municipal court and no preliminary hearing would occur.

Shortly before the trial date, a docket sounding occurs to let attorneys announce if they are ready for trial. A docket sounding is a conference between the judge, defense attorney, and prosecuting attorney. If they are not ready for the trial, they must state their reasons. The trial date is frequently extended to allow for additional preparation.[9]

If there is enough evidence and the accused pleaded innocent at the preliminary hearing, an actual *trial* will be held several months later. During the trial, evidence will be presented by both the prosecution and the defense. Witnesses testify during the trial.

During the sentencing phase, while the probation department is making its report, the probation officer may require a physical lie detector test of the perpetrator's responses to various visual/auditory stimuli. It has been said that the body never lies.

3. Relative Outside the Home

Other children in the family may have been victimized as well. With legal follow-through, it is relatively easy to protect the victim and other children from further victimization. Follows the same process as for Neighbor/Friend.

4. Relative Inside the Home

A relative living inside the home could include a father, stepfather, sibling, cousin, or other relative. In this case, the adult perpetrator may be required to move out of the home for a period of time, and would most likely accept a plea bargain, with required counseling for all family members.

The perpetrator's attitude and cooperation help to determine whether the child may be released to the mother or taken into protective custody. Particularly in cases of father-daughter incest, interviews—after proper legal cautioning—by a pair (preferably female and male) of police detectives who are not in uniform and preferably in the perpetrator's home, lead to rapid confession in many cases.

This works effectively when legal criminal bypass procedures exist in the county. In such jurisdictions, the district attorney and the child protective service authorities join the perpetrator in signing a contract which includes the requirement of not less than two years of treatment. Certain perpetrators, such as violent offenders, are automatically ineligible for this program. Violent offenders, along with those who do not admit to the offense, constitute a minority. [10]

Some incest cases never go to criminal court. You may work with a family court judge who believes in the family and feels that your family can be rebuilt. He may issue court orders and instructions towards the goal of healing, rather than punishing. [11]

If the perpetrator is a brother or sister who is a minor, this issue would be handled through the juvenile court system, after reporting it to the police. Counseling would be required for all family members. Follows the same process as for Neighbor/Friend.

5. *Father with Visitation*

Protecting a child from a father who has visitation rights without legal follow-through in two court systems can be extremely difficult. You may be required to go through two court actions at once. The first would be family court to get protection through a change in the custody/visitation order. The second court action would be through the criminal court system.

Some agencies offer a support system during this time. One woman I know who went through the legal process was assisted by an organization called Bay Area Women Against Rape. Someone from this organization was with her during the legal process. Rape Crisis Centers listed in the yellow pages of your phone directory would be a good resource for information. Check to see what's available in your area.

Please note that the family court mediator may not believe the evidence of molestation, making it absolutely necessary to go through the criminal justice system. Whether the perpetrator plea bargains or goes to successful trial, the child will be protected for the length of sentence, plus probation, plus however long it takes for successful completion of a sex offender counseling program.

Should My Child Testify?

One of the most frequently asked questions I receive from parents is "Should my child testify?" Unfortunately, there is not one simple answer. The most important consideration is the child himself. Some children need to testify as part of their healing process. For some children though, testifying could be more damaging. Caring parents and adults, who know the child personally, can best make this vital decision. Whether the child testifies or not, remember that no judge will be able to erase the memories of the sexual abuse.

Some studies have found that child sexual abuse victims who participate in judicial proceedings suffer more harm than children who do not go to court, although there is little direct evidence of exactly which aspect of the court experience causes the trauma.[12]

Last year, our younger daughter was hit by a car. It was important for her recovery to be involved in the reporting and investigation of the accident. Due to her age, she was not required by the police department or insurance company to give a report. She chose to give the police a report and participate in the insurance investigation. I felt that her involvement gave her closure to the event and made the accident more believable since adults listened to her side of the story. Repeating the story also helped her realize that she was not responsible for the accident.

Twenty states have followed the federal rules of evidence by presuming competence of all persons to testify, including children. The Attorney General's Task Force of Family Violence (September 1984) urges that "children, regardless of their age, should be presumed to be competent to testify in court. A child's testimony should be allowed into evidence with credibility being determined by the jury."[13]

As an adult, ask, "What is the child's ability to accurately perceive events, remember them, and communicate them accurately?" Keep in mind that children often report more limited information than do adults, but what they report can be just as accurate.[14]

Assisting the Child Witness

Children may be twice victimized, once by the abuser and once by the court system. Recently, there has been an emphasis on helping children to feel comfortable in court. Some states have permitted closed-circuit television in the hopes of lessening the stress of the victim who is testifying. Videotaping testimonies is another controversial technique. Videotapes taken at a deposition or preliminary hearing are allowed in at least fourteen states as substitutes for live testimony at the trial.

Some of the most useful techniques in making a child victim of sexual abuse feel comfortable during the trial are simple and can be easily implemented. Consider providing a small chair for the child in the courtroom. The judge can sit on a level with the child and possibly even wear business clothes instead of a robe. Someone from the court should explain what is going on to the child. The child can be allowed to sit in the witness chair in the courtroom and use the microphone.[15] Professionals suggest the number of spectators allowed in courtroom during a child's testimony be reduced to make testifying easier for the child.

Various states have passed statutes allowing and encouraging the use of a support person at the trial for the child witness. This support person can be a relative, a friend, or a witness assistance person hired by the court who will stay with the child through all the phases of the court process. The child can have this support person near during the testimony and may even sit on the person's lap, if desired.[16]

Children's responses to testifying will vary. One child said,

> I felt like Mommy was right, that we had to do it. We had to make sure he wasn't going to hurt any other little girls. I hated it. I had to tell the story over and over and over again to so many people. The day that it was over they let him plead guilty to a lesser charge. He was sentenced to six months. All I kept thinking about after I heard this was that it had taken more than six months already. That meant he was going to be out really soon, and I wasn't really protecting anybody. I kept asking my mother why did I have to go through this. He'd be out before we knew it.[17]

One mother said,

> During this trying period, my daughter felt that she had no one
> to turn to. I didn't know how much she was afraid of being sent
> to a foster home, or how isolated she felt. When she later joined
> a therapy group, she discovered that many girls in this predica-
> ment are afraid that they might be thrown out of their home by
> their mother, or taken away by the authorities.[18]

One helpful resource book written for children is *Margaret's
Story—Sexual Abuse and Going to Court.* (Deborah Anderson
and Martha Finne, Illus. Jeanette Swofford, Minneapolis, Minn:
Dillon Press, Inc., 1986.) This book describes the experiences
of a young girl who is sexually abused by her neighbor and
what happens when she seeks help. It also includes a glossary
of terms and sources of help for abused children.

Alternatives to Child Testimony

If a case goes to trial, it may be possible to proceed without
having to call the child as a witness in court. Several exceptions
to the hearsay rule may be applicable. The most common
ones are excited utterance (Federal Rules of Evidence 803(2))
and statements made in the course of medical examination
(Federal Rule of Evidence 803(4)). A number of states have
created special exceptions to the hearsay rule for child sexual
abuse victims. The state of Washington allows admission of a
reported statement by a child under ten, which would otherwise be inadmissible, if the statement provides sufficient indications of reliability and either the child testifies at the
proceedings or the child is unavailable, and there is corrobora-
tive evidence of the fact (Wash, Rev. Code 9A.44.120).[19]

While hearsay evidence is generally not admitted in criminal
cases, an exception is now emerging in American law practice
when a child complains to any third party about sexual abuse.
These circumstances are now occasionally allowed as ad-
missible evidence.

Recently some appeals courts have ruled in either civil or criminal cases that another person may fully testify to the child's complaints, and that this is not 'unduly prejudicial and is highly convincing,' a giant step forward because it means that the young victim may not have to appear in court and retell these events in public at all.[20]

Conviction of Perpetrators

The convicted molester can receive a jail sentence, a period of probation, and/or mandatory treatment. Only one out of one hundred molesters is apprehended and of these, only 1 out of ten is convicted. The maximum sentence for child molesting is eight years.[21]

"Sex abusers have the lowest conviction rate of any crime. DeVine reported in 1978 that only one in every sixty reported cases resulted in a conviction. Those convicted served an average of less than twelve months in jail."[22] In communities where time pressures on child protective services is very great, sometimes the authorities resort to "three months of family therapy" and the early closing of the case. These cases have a very high rate of recidivism, depriving the victim of protection.[23]

In one diversion program, the offender must plead guilty to the charge to be included in the program. This requirement is vital to the program's success. Guilt, once admitted, can be accepted and made truly therapeutic resulting in improved self-esteem and the beginning of insights which lead to successful treatment of the family, the victim, and the offender in most cases. Without an admission of guilt, little change is possible because denial totally blocks the path toward understanding and often makes the offender feel that he has "fooled the system."[24]

This chapter has given you an overview of the legal system. Be sure to contact authorities in your area to get specific information. As we near the end of this book, let's look at what we've experienced through the tears.

11

Through the Tears

Thou tellest my wanderings; put thou my tears into thy
bottle: are they not in thy book?
(Ps. 56:8)

April 4, 1989: It's so beautiful here at Campus Cru-
sade for Christ's headquarters in Arrowhead Springs,
near San Bernardino. God's timing is amazing. A year
ago, I was here, devastated, as I recognized the symptoms of sexual abuse in my daughter.

Now, just one year later, I have hope. I'm here for a
women's retreat, but this time I won't be listening to a
speaker on sexual abuse; I will be speaking on sexual
abuse. For the first time, I will be recounting my story of
discovering my own sexual abuse. There will still be
rough waters ahead, but I've seen so many miracles,
especially in the past ten days. Only God could have
prepared the perpetrator for the confrontation. Only
God could reveal truth and bring about healing.

As I sit outside praying, I'm looking onto the San
Bernardino Valley. I watch the lizards scurrying about.
Since I really don't like lizards, I check to see if there
are any near me. Then I focus back on praying to God.

Soon, out of the corner of my eye, another lizard
catches my attention again and distracts my prayer

time. I guess that's my story with God. I do fine with my focus on God for a time, and then I get distracted by lizards. The lizards in my life can be problems, circumstances, or people. I find myself torn between focusing on lizards and focusing on God (*Journal entry*)

When I wasn't distracted by the lizards, I sat in the warm sun and wrote in my journal. I imagined a person in San Bernardino looking up towards Arrowhead Springs. The mountain must seem very far away when you're in the valley. On some days, the mountain can't even be seen because of the smog. That's often my perspective as a Christian. I see life through the smog. The picture is not clear nor is it pretty.

Yet when I look down from the mountain, I can see the whole valley. I remind myself that this is somewhat like God's view. He sees the entire picture of our lives, not just the valley through the smog.

As you've read this book through your own tears, I trust you have been able to learn and apply some of the information to your own circumstances. Nehemiah 8:10 says, "Do not grieved, for the joy of the Lord is your strength" (NASB). I could not have walked through this valley without a personal friendship with my best Friend in the entire world, Jesus Christ. I prayed for a sense of peace, calm, wisdom, and direction on many occasions.

After I confronted the perpetrator and his wife, she said they were sorry they had ruined my life. I assured her that they hadn't ruined my life. God was using it for good. In the Old Testament, a young man named Joseph was sold into slavery by his own brothers.

Years later, he became a high-ranking official in Pharaoh's court. Genesis 50:20 says, "You intended to harm me, but God intended it for good to accomplish what is now being done."

God can bring good into your life through any circumstances, but He must be given that opportunity. Perhaps you do not know the healer of all tears, Jesus Christ. Will you decide to begin a personal relationship with Christ? Will you allow God to heal your life? Or will you continue to remain bitter, angry, hopeless, and unable to forgive the perpetrator(s)?

If you would like to receive Jesus Christ, by faith, you can express your desire through prayer. Prayer is simply talking to God. You may use words of your own or use this suggested prayer.

"Dear God, I know that my sin has separated me from you. Thank you that Jesus Christ died in my place. I ask Jesus to forgive my sin and to come into my life. Please begin to direct my life. Thank you for giving me eternal life. In Jesus' name, Amen."

If you have decided to make a commitment to Jesus Christ, please tell a Christian friend or a pastor at a church. If you would like more information on this life-changing decision, please write to me in care of Broadman Press, Nashville, TN 37234.

Only God can restore dreams and shattered lives. As I write the conclusion of my book, I am fulfilling two dreams. Over nine years ago, I decided to write a book. I didn't know what I'd write about or when I'd have the opportunity, but God has allowed me to accomplish a dream.

Another dream I had was to own a beach house where I could write as I overlook the ocean. This evening, I am writing as I overlook the ocean. The house isn't mine, but maybe someday I will have an oceanfront home! But for today, I have these moments of pleasure and hope for future dreams.

Just as the ocean changes every day with a low tide and a high tide, our lives are constantly changing every day. Some days we experience low days when our lives seem covered with clouds, dreariness, and darkness. Some days reflect the sun and radiate our lives with joy, warmth, and happiness. We do not know what God holds in store for each of us every day.

What I do know, is that God has a purpose and plan for my daughter, my family, and myself.

As I gazed out onto the ocean, and it became totally dark, I reflected on the many days that looked black to me and I didn't feel any hope. I recalled the days I felt defeated and wondered if my daughter would ever be emotionally healthy. I wondered if she'd ever finish counseling. I remembered the times I wondered if I'd ever be able to make a simple request without fearing she would turn it into a major uphill battle.

Would she ever be happy and not angry? Would she ever really love her sister and not continually resent her? Would there be a day when she didn't keep score and protest, "It's not fair?"

On many occasions, I wondered what she'd think of her father and me when she grows up. Would she blame us for not being good parents, or would she appreciate how hard we tried? Would she realize how much love, time, and energy we spent trying to be the best parents we could possibly be for her?

I already know the answers to some of these questions because God has given me rays of hope. As the sun rises in the morning and begins to reflect and glisten off the ocean, I have seen glimmers of hope in my daughter's life. I watch for these moments with great anticipation because they give me the courage and strength to persist in parenting. God always seems to know when I need a moment when the tears stream down my face, not with hurt and pain, but with joy and hope.

In the introduction to this book, I suggested that you keep a journal of the recovery process. Recently, I've read through all my journals to make sure I communicated what I wanted to include. As I read, I noticed that many pages were stained with tears. Some were tears from when I originally wrote the journal entry. Some of the pages had fresh tears as I reread the journals and cried, reflecting on the progress and healing I'd seen.

I would never choose to go though the painful circumstances of sexual abuse for my daughter, my family, or myself. Even though I still have many questions and missing puzzle pieces, I do know that God has changed her life, my family's lives, and my own life, Through the Tears. I pray God will heal your precious child's life through your tears.

Bibliography

Suggested Books for Preschool Children

A Better Safe than Sorry Book: A Family Guide for Sexual Assault Prevention, Sol and Judith Gordon, illus. by Vivien Cohen (Fayetteville, NY: Ed-U Press, Inc, 1984). Ages three to nine. Helps children feel better about themselves. Provides essential information about sexual assault. Includes parent's guide.

It's My Body, Lory Freeman, illus. by Carol Deach (Seattle, Wash.: Parenting Press, Inc, 1982, twenty-four pages). Different situations help children distinguish between appropriate and inappropriate touching and how to respond. A parent's resource guide is also available.

It's OK to Say No, Amy C. Bahr, illus. by Frederick Bennet Green (New York: Grosset and Dunlap, 1986). Discusses what to do if approached by a stranger or if someone touches you in an uncomfortable way.

Sometimes It's OK to Tell Secrets, Amy C. Bahr, illus. by Frederick Bennet Green (New York: Grosset and Dunlap, 1986).

What Should You Do When...? Amy C. Bahr, illus. by Frederick Bennet Green (New York: Grosset and Dunlap, 1986).

Suggested Books for School-age Children

Help Yourself to Safety—A Guide to Avoiding Dangerous Situations with Strangers and Friends, Kate Hubbard and Evelyn Berlin. Illus. by Marina Megale (Edmonds, Wash.: The Chas. Franklin Press, 1985, thirty-two pages). Assists child in how to be protected against molestation and abduction. Includes safety tips for adults and children.

It's Not Your Fault, Judith A. Jance. Illus. by Marina Megale (Edmonds, Wash.: The Chas. Franklin Press, 1985, eighteen pages.) This book gives a clear message: you are not to blame, and it is good that you told. Includes discussion questions.

It's O.K. to Say No! A Parent/Child Manual for the Protection of Children, Robin Lenett and Bob Crane. Illus. by Frank C. Smith (New York: RGA Publishing Group Inc. and Frank Smith, 1985, 128 pages). First five chapters for parents, followed by stories to read with children.

Let's Talk About It, Margaret O. Hyde (Philadelphia: Westminster, 1984). A book to help children understand what sexual abuse is, what to do if it happens, why they should not feel guilty, where to go for help, and what will happen when they seek help.

No More Secrets for Me, Oralee Wachter, illus. by Jane Aaron (Boston, Mass.: Little, Brown and Company, 1983, forty-seven pages). Four stories about children facing exploitive situations. The book emphasizes the child's right to say "no" and encourages confiding in a trusted adult.

My Body Is Private, Linda Walvoord Girard, illus. by Rodney Pate (Niles, Ill.: Albert Whitman and Co, 1984). A mother-child conversation introduces the topic of sexual abuse and ways to keep one's body private.

Private Zone—A Book Teaching Children Sexual Assault Prevention Tools, Frances S. Dayee. Illus. by Marina Megale (Edmonds, Wash.: The Chas. Franklin Press, 1982). Emphasizing the concept of privacy, Dayee discusses who may touch the child's body and under what circumstances. Included is information for parents about sexual assault.

Something Happened to Me, Phyllis E. Sweet, illus, by Barbara Lindquist (Racine, Wis.: Mother Courage Press, 1981). This book encourages the child to speak, rather than carrying a guilty and fearful secret.

Who Is a Stranger and What Should I Do? Linda Walvoord Girard, illus. by Helen Cogancherry (Niles, Ill.: Albert Whitman and Co, 1985, thirty-one pages.) Explains how to deal with strangers in public places, on the telephone, and in cars, emphasizing situations in which the best thing to do is run away or talk to another adult. Includes practice situations.

Suggested Books for Adolescents

Safe, Strong, & Streetwise—Sexual Safety at Home, On the Street, On Dates, On the Job, At Parties, & More, Helen Benedict (Boston: Little, Brown and Company, 1987). Educates teenagers about what sexual assault is, how to avoid it, and how not to do it to anyone else. It does not promote abstinence until marriage.

Self-esteem Resources

Children

Pizza for Everyone, Josh & Dottie McDowell, illus. by Meredith Johnson, (Elgin, Ill.: Chariot Books, David C. Cook, 1988).

Eekebee, Yes That's Me! Jack Pearson, illus. by Kent Mockintosh (Elgin, Ill.: Chariot Books, David C. Cook, 1989).

Teens

Listening to My Heart, Eva Gibson (Minneapolis, Minn.: Bethany House Publishers, 1990). Gives journaling help to girls (ages eleven to fourteen) struggling with new, intense feelings of self-discovery. Guides readers into an open relationship with God as their best friend and confidant.

That Very Special Person—Me! Margaret Houk (Scottsdale, Penn.: Herald Press, 1990). Young teens take a personal inventory and appreciate what they see in themselves. Readers get tips on identifying negative messages, checking them out with reliable sources, and substituting constructive ways of thinking.

So What's Wrong with A Big Nose? Fran and Jill Sciacca (Lifelines Studies, Colorado Springs, Col.: Nav Press, 1988).

Self Image: Learning to Like Yourself, Bill Jones (San Bernardino, Calif.: Here's Life Publishers, 1988).

Teen Pregnancy Resources

Daddy, I'm Pregnant, author: a dad named Bill, (Portland, Ore.: Multnomah Press, 1987).

Handbook for Pregnant Teenagers, Linda Roggow and Carolyn Owens, (Grand Rapids, Mich.: Zondervan, 1985). This book is excellent but out of print. Perhaps you could borrow a copy.

Just Like Ice Cream, Lissa Halls Johnson, (Palm Springs: Calif.: R.N. Hayes, 1985). When sixteen-year old Julie discovers that she is pregnant, she is genuinely surprised and confused. Written from a teenager's viewpoint, this novel takes the glamour and mystique out of sexual promiscuity.

Should I Keep My Baby? Martha Zimmerman (Waco, Tex.: Word Publishing, 1983).

Notes

Chapter 1

1. Jennifer Fay, "He Told Me Not to Tell," King County Rape Relief, Renton, Wash., (1979), 16.

2. Kathryn B. Hagans and Joyce Case, *When Your Child Has Been Molested: A Parents Guide to Healing and Recovery; Putting the Pieces Back Together* (Lexington, Mass.: Lexington Books, 1988), 20.

3. Jeffrey J. Jaugaard and N. Dickon Reppucci, *The Sexual Abuse of Children* (San Francisco, Calif.: Jossey-Bass Publishers, 1988), 193.

4. *Child Sexual Abuse: Incest, Assault and Sexual Exploitation* (U.S. Department of Health, Education and Welfare, publication 79-30266), 2.

5. Hagans and Case, 40.

6. John Crewdson, *By Silence Betrayed: Sexual Abuse of Children in America* (Boston: Little, Brown, 1988), 208.

7. *Basic Facts About Child Sexual Abuse*, 3d ed. (1988), 5.

8. C. Henry Kempe and Ruth S. Kempe, *The Common Secret: Sexual Abuse of Children and Adolescents* (New York: W.H. Freeman and Co., 1984), 10.

9. See Crewdson, 26-27, and Lloyd Martin and Jill Haddad, *We Have a Secret* (Newport Beach, Calif.: Crown Summit Books, 1982), 3.

10. Kempe and Kempe, *The Common Secret*, 11.

11. Ibid.

12. Crewdson, 26-27.

13. Kempe and Kempe, *The Common Secret*, 11-13.

14. Ibid., 13.

15. Margaret O. Hyde, *Sexual Abuse: Let's Talk About It* (Philadelphia: Westminster Press, 1987), 35.

16. *Basic Facts About Child Sexual Abuse*, 9.

17. Elaine Landau, *Child Abuse: An American Epidemic* (New York: Julian Messner, 1984), 62.

18. Kempe and Kempe, *The Common Secret*, 17.

Chapter 2

1. Martin and Haddad, 7.

2. Diane D. Broakhurst, Philip E. Fox, and Donald F. Kline, *Children Alone* (Renton, Wash.: The Council for Exceptional Children, 1977), 45.

3. Ibid., 46.

4. Ibid., 47.

5. Ibid., 48.

6. Ibid., 49.

7. Haugaard and Reppucci, 151.

8. Ibid., 151-52.

9. Flora Colao and Tamar Hosansky, *Your Children Should Know* (Indianapolis: The Bobbs-Merrill Co., 1983), 126.

10. Haugaard and Reppucci, 155.

11. Ibid., 153.

12. Reprinted from *Child Sexual Abuse: A Hope for Healing* (p. 164), c 1987 by Maxine Hancock and Karen Mains. Used by permission of Harold Shaw Publishers, Wheaton, IL.

13. David Finkelhor, *Sexually Victimized Children* (New York: The Free Press, 1987), ch. 7.

14. Karin C. Meiselman, *Incest: A Psychological Study of Causes and Effects with Treatment Recommendations* (San Francisco, Calif.: Jossey-Bass, 1978), 186.

15. Tamar Cohen, "The Incestuous Family Revisited," *So-*

cial Casework: The Journal of Contemporary Social Work (March 1983): 158.

16. The fourth, fifth, and sixth factors are from Kempe and Kempe, 112-13.

17. Jaugaard and Reppucci, 85-86.

Chapter 3

1. Dennis Linn and Matthew Linn, *Healing Life's Hurts: Healing Memories Through the Five Stages of Forgiveness* (New York: Paulist Press, 1978), 91.

2. Ibid., 88-89.

3. David A. Seamands, *Healing for Damaged Emotions* (Wheaton, Ill.: Victor Books, 1988), 106.

4. Nancy O'Connor, *Letting Go with Love: The Grieving Process* (Tucson, Ariz.: La Mariposa Press, 1984), 37.

5. Ann Kaiser Stearns, *Living Through Personal Crisis* (Chicago: The Thomas More Press, 1984), 37.

6. James Dobson, *Hide or Seek* (Old Tappan, N.J.: Fleming H. Revell, 1974), 66.

7. Ibid.

8. Gail McDonald, *High Call, High Privilege* (Wheaton, Ill.: Tyndale House Publishers), 168.

9. Linn and Linn, 164.

10. Marilyn Willett Heavilin, *December's Song* (San Bernardino, Calif.: Here's Life Publishers, 1988), 50.

11. Joni Eareckson Tada and Steve Estes, *A Step Further* (Grand Rapids, Mich.: Zondervan Publishing House, 1978), 15-16.

12. Information about personality temperaments is from Marilyn Willett Heavilin, *Roses in December* (San Bernardino, Calif.: Here's Life Publishers, 1986), 22-23, 107-8.

13. S. I. McMillen, *None of These Diseases* (Westwood, N. J.: Fleming H. Revell Co., 1963), 73-74.

14. Lewis Smedes, *Forgive and Forget* (San Francisco, Calif.: Harper and Row, 1984).

15. Lewis Smedes, "Forgiveness: Healing the Hurts We Don't Deserve," *Family Life Today*, January 1985, 24-28.

Chapter 4

1. Martin and Haddad, 127.

2. Donna Gaffney, *The Seasons of Grief: Helping Your Children Grow Through Loss* (New York: New American Library, 1988), 78.

3. Robert L. Veninga, "How to Cope with Heartache," *Ladies Home Journal*, November 1985, 74-82.

4. Jaugaard and Reppucci, 150.

5. Jean Goodwin, et. al., *Sexual Abuse: Incest Victims and Their Families* (Boston, John Wright—PSG, 1982), 6.

6. Information on true and false accusations is based on Jaugaard and Reppucci, 157, 174-76.

7. Patty Derosier Barnes, *The Woman Inside, from Incest Victim to Survivor* (Racine, Wis.: Mother Courage Press, 1989), 13.

8. Goodwin, 66-67.

9. Ray E. Helfer and Ruth S. Kempe, *The Battered Child*, 4th ed. (Chicago: The University of Chicago Press, 1987), 355.

10. Goodwin, 71-72.

11. Reprinted from *Child Sexual Abuse: A Hope for Healing* (p. 135), c 1987 by Maxine Hancock and Karen Mains. Used by permission of Harold Shaw Publishers, Wheaton, IL.

12. Hagans and Case, 137.

13. According to Alexander G. Zaphiris, one hour weekly treatment sessions for two to three years can ensure a comprehensive and permanent outcome. See Zaphiris, "Father-Daughter Incest," in *Sexual Abuse of Children: Implications for Treatment* (Colorado Child Protection Division, 1983), 90.

Chapter 5

1. One excellent resource is a series of six Christian books, *Learning About Sex—A Series for the Christian Family* (St.

Louis, Missouri: Concordia Publishing House, 1982.) The first five books are written for various age groups of children, beginning with *Why Boys and Girls Are Different* by Carol Greene, written for three- to five-year-olds. We are currently using *How You Are Changing* by Jane Graver, written for children ages eight to eleven and *Sex and the New You* by Richard Bimler, written for ages eleven to fourteen. The last book in the series, *How to Talk Confidently with Your Child about Sex* by Lenore Buth is written for parents. This book helps adults deal with their own sexuality and provides practical assistance for married and single parents in their role as sex educators in the home.

Another book our family used in the area of sex education is *The Wonderful Way that Babies Are Made* by Larry Christenson. (Minneapolis, Minn.: Bethany House Publishers, 1982.) This book is written on two levels. First, it's written on a simple level for a parent to read aloud to young children. The pictures and the large print are designed for children ages three to eight. The second level is written for an older child to read to himself. The smaller-print paragraphs on each page give additional information for children ages nine to fourteen.

James Dobson's *Preparing for Adolescence* is an excellent resource for educating young people about puberty and sexuality. (Ventura, Calif.: Regal Books, 1978, 1989.) A family tape set is available. The two parent tapes include guidelines for parents on what to expect and what to say. The six youth tapes are friendly discussions that are spoken directly to teens.

When my daughter began puberty, the two of us went away for the weekend. My mom had given us some money for our time together. We listened to the tapes together and discussed what she learned. Hopefully, I provided an open and fun environment in which she could learn and ask questions. We both enjoyed this milestone in her life.

Another book for preadolescents is *Almost 12—The Story of Sex* by Kenneth N. Taylor. (Wheaton, Ill.: Tyndale House, 1989.)

If you have teenagers, you will want to know about the "Why Wait?" series designed for parents and teenagers. *Teens Speak Out: "What I Wish My Parents Knew About My Sexuality"* by Josh McDowell (San Bernardino, Calif.: Here's Life Publishers, 1987.) is comprised primarily of responses from teenagers indicating what they are thinking and feeling in the area of sexuality. Also in this series are three excellent books by Barry St. Clair and Bill Jones for your teenager: *Dating: Picking (and Being) a Winner*, *Sex: Desiring the Best*, and *Love: Making It Last.* You can go through these books with your teens or have them read the books, and discuss them together. A "Why Wait?" video series called "No! The Positive Answer" (Waco, Tex.: Word Inc., 1988) is also available. This video series includes four thirty-minute sessions for teenagers.

I hope you will find these resources helpful as you begin to communicate with your child about sex. Eventually, your children will get information on sex. Wouldn't you rather have them hear about sex from you?

2. Jaugaard and Reppucci, 227.

3. Judith Cooney, *Coping with Sexual Abuse* (New York: The Rosen Publishing Group, 1987), 82.

4. Ruth S. Kempe and C. Henry Kempe, *Child Abuse* in *The Developing Child Series* (Cambridge: Harvard University Press, 1978), 53-54.

Chapter 6

1. Sherryll Kerns Kraizer, *The Safe Child Book* (New York: Delacorte Press, 1985), 45.

2. Helen Benedict, *Safe, Strong, and Streetwise* (Boston: Little, Brown and Co., 1987), 167-68.

3. Danalee Buhler, *The Very Best Child Care and How to Find It* (Rocklin, Calif.: Prima Publishing and Communications, 1989), 124.

4. Based on Dawn C. Haden, *Out of Harm's Way,* 109, reprinted from Ann French Clark and Jane Bingham, "The

Play Technique: Diagnosing the Sexually Abused Child,"
Tarrant County Physician, August 1984.

5. Linda Tschirhart Sanford, *The Silent Children: A Parent's Guide to the Prevention of Child Sexual Abuse* (Lebanon, N. H.: McGraw-Hill Book Co., 1980), 146.

6. Cynthia Crosson Tower, *Secret Scars: A Guide for Survivors of Child Sexual Abuse* (New York: Viking Penguin, 1988), 161.

7. Based on Dawn C. Haden, *Out of Harm's Way*, 109-10, reprinted from Ann French Clark and Jane Bingham, "The Play Technique: Diagnosing the Sexually Abused Child," *Tarrant County Physician*, August 1984.

8. Barnes, 77.

9. Kempe and Kempe, *The Common Secret*, 165.

10. Goodwin, 89.

11. Helfer and Kempe, *The Battered Child*, 375-76.

12. Based on Dawn C. Haden, *Out of Harm's Way*, 110, reprinted from Ann French Clark and Jane Bingham, "The Play Technique: Diagnosing the Sexually Abused Child," *Tarrant County Physician*, August 1984.

13. Colao and Hosansky, 113.

14. Ibid.

15. See Benedict, 171-73.

Chapter 7

1. See Dawn C. Haden, *Out of Harm's Way*, 102, reprinted from Ann French Clark and Jane Bingham, "The Play Technique: Diagnosing the Sexually Abused Child," *Tarrant County Physician*, August 1984.

2. Kevin Leman and Randy Carlson, *Unlocking the Secrets of Your Childhood Memories* (Nashville, Tenn.: Thomas Nelson Publishers, 1989), 167.

3. Ibid., 213-14.

4. Merton P. Strommen and A. Irene Strommen, *Five*

Cries of Parents (San Francisco, Calif.: Harper and Row, 1985), 187.

5. Dobson, 160.

6. The following information on anger in children is based on Donna Miller, *Mothers and Others Be Aware* (Burbank, Calif.: Restauration Books, 1985), 113-15.

7. Cited in H. Norman Wright, *Beating the Blues* (Ventura, Calif.: Regal Books, 1988), 38.

8. H. Norman Wright, *Crisis Counseling: Helping People in Crisis and Stress* (San Bernardino, Calif.: Here's Life Publishers, 1985), 76-77.

9. Dianne Hales, *The Encyclopedia of Health*, s.v. "Psychological Disorders and Their Treatment, Depression."

10. Gaffney, 87-88. Several charts in Joel Herskowitz, *Is Your Child Depressed?* (New York: Warner Books, 1988), may help you identify depression in your child or a child that you're concerned about.

11. Marion Duckworth, *Why Teens Are Killing Themselves and What We Can Do About It* (San Bernardino, Calif.: Here's Life Publishers, 1987), 36-39.

12. Ibid., 14-15.

13. Hales, 64-65.

14. See ibid., 70, and Wright, *Crisis Counseling*, 106.

15. Goodwin, 114.

Chapter 8

1. Mark A. Stewart and Sally Wendkos Olds, *Raising a Hyperactive Child* (New York: Harper and Row, 1973), 3.

2. Herskowitz, 187-88.

3. Richard Bardrick, "Attention Deficit Disorder/Hyperactivity," *Rapha Insights*, vol 1, no. 7.

4. Terence J. Sandbek, *The Deadly Diet: Recovering from Anorexia and Bulimia* (Oakland, Calif.: New Harbinger Publications, 1986), 24.

5. Patricia A. Newman and Patricia A. Halvorson, *Anorexia*

Nervosa and Bulimia: A Handbook for Counselors and Therapists (New York: Van Nostrand Reinhold Co., 1983), 2.

6. Jane Claypool Minev and Cheryl Diane Nelsen, *Food Trips and Traps: Coping with Eating Disorders* (New York: Franklin Watts, 1983), 14-15.

7. Newman and Halvorson, 40.

8. Sandbek, 25.

9. Strommen and Strommen, 57.

10. Ibid., 179.

11. Miller, 117.

12. Landau, 64.

Chapter 9

1. Sanford, 171.

2. Ibid., 13.

3. Dobson, 79.

4. Charlie Shedd, ed., *You Are Somebody Special* (New York: McGraw-Hill, 1978), 125-26.

5. Dorothy Corkille Briggs, *Your Child's Self-esteem* (Garden City, N. Y.: Doubleday and Co., 1970), xiv.

6. Leman and Carlson, 89.

7. Ibid., 89-92.

8. H. Norman Wright, *The Power of a Parent's Words* (Ventura, Calif.: Regal Books, 1991), 241-42.

9. Shedd, 93.

10. Dobson, 97.

11. Tower, 142.

12. Quoted in ibid., 141.

13. Tower, 141.

14. Miller

15. Ibid., 102.

16. Shedd, 73.

17. Barbara Varenhorst, *Real Friends: Becoming the Friend You'd Like to Have* (San Francisco: Harper and Row, 1984).

Chapter 10

1. Miller, 47.
2. Kempe and Kempe, *The Common Secret*, 91.
3. Ibid., 84-85.
4. Colao and Hosansky, 133.
5. Ibid.
6. Miller, 53.
7. Hagans and Case, 14-16.
8. Miller, 53.
9. Hagans and Case, 16.
10. Kempe and Kempe, *The Common Secret*, 88.
11. Hagans and Case, 137.
12. Helfer and Kempe, 415.
13. Ibid., 416.
14. Ibid.
15. Hyde, 66-67.
16. Helfer and Kempe, 417.
17. Colao and Hosansky, 135.
18. Miller, 38-39.
19. Helfer and Kempe, 418.
20. Kempe and Kempe, *The Common Secret*, 85.
21. "Some Facts on Child Molestation," Parents United paper.
22. Kraizer, 116.
23. Kempe and Kempe, *The Common Secret*, 89.
24. Ibid., 90.